~~48~~ ~~12~~ MORE RULES

FOR LIFE

A SPECIAL VOLUME FOR ENTHUSIASTS

REBECCA BANA

ABOUT THE AUTHOR

Kitty Flanagan is one of Australia's best-known comedians. She appears on TV occasionally but spends most of her time touring the country doing stand-up.

She has two dogs, one cat and a dishwasher that she loves more than all of her pets combined. Her favourite food is soup. *More Rules for Life* is her third book.

Also by Kitty Flanagan

Bridge Burning & other hobbies—
a collection of funny true stories

488 Rules for Life:
The thankless art of being correct

~~488~~ ~~12~~ MORE RULES

FOR LIFE

A SPECIAL VOLUME FOR ENTHUSIASTS

KITTY FLANAGAN

with fellow rule-makers
Sophie Braham & Penny Flanagan

Illustrations by Tohby Riddle

ALLEN&UNWIN
SYDNEY • MELBOURNE • AUCKLAND • LONDON

Neither the author nor the publisher has any connection with either Jordan Peterson, the author of *12 Rules for Life*, or the publisher of that book, and readers must not interpret anything in this book as giving rise to any such connection.

First published in 2021

Allen & Unwin
83 Alexander Street
Crows Nest NSW 2065
Australia
Phone: (61 2) 8425 0100
Email: info@allenandunwin.com
Web: www.allenandunwin.com

 A catalogue record for this book is available from the National Library of Australia

ISBN 978 1 76106 661 0

Internal design and illustrations by Tohby Riddle
Index by Garry Cousins
Set in 10.8/18.1 pt Interstate by Bookhouse, Sydney
Printed and bound in Australia by Griffin Press, part of Ovato

10 9 8 7 6 5 4 3 2 1

 The paper in this book is FSC® certified. FSC® promotes environmentally responsible, socially beneficial and economically viable management of the world's forests.

*For Jazzy, my long-suffering,
rule-abiding unicorn xx*

Contents

A word from the author   xi

How to use this book   xiii

THIS & THAT   1

Leisure and lifestyle   3

House and garden   5

Holidays and travel   8

COMING OF AGE   11

A word about my generation   13

Generation X   15

Baby Boomers   19

Millennials   23

Generation Z   26

PANDEMIC TIMES—THE BASICS   29

SHOP TALK   37

Consumers   39

Retailers   42

Cafes   44

CLEAR COMMUNICATION 47

Texting and emailing 49

Kids party invitations 52

Language 53

PANDEMIC TIMES—MASKS 59

FOOD STUFF 65

Eating 67

Cooking 69

A word about the Christmas menu 71

Recipe websites 73

The great outdoors 75

THE ART OF ENTERTAINMENT 77

Podcasts 79

Reality television 83

A word about the arts industry 86

Friends of the show 88

Zoom gigs 90

PANDEMIC TIMES—ZOOM ETIQUETTE 91

SOCIALISING 99

Catching up 101

Furry friends 103

Meeting and greeting 105

Special follow-up rule for the married ladies 108

Sexy taimes 109

PANDEMIC TIMES—SOME SPECIFICS   111

AND FINALLY . . .   115

    Some strong suggestions   117
    And one stupid suggestion   119

Acknowledgements   121
Index to *488 Rules for Life* and
More Rules for Life   123

A word from the author

When *488 Rules for Life* was published, I thought I had covered everything. About a week later, new rules started popping into my head and I realised I still had so much more to give. Then Covid-19 hit and the world spiralled out of control. There were no rules for a pandemic, the government was floundering and I knew I had to step up. So that's what this book is: rules I forgot the first time, rules for the grave new world we're living in, plus some rules I considered a little too savage for the original book. *More Rules for Life* is for true aficionados, people who want and appreciate boundaries; it's not for easygoing folks with a 'whatever will be, will be' attitude. The warning is on the cover, this is a book for enthusiasts.

How to use this book

It may have been a while since you read *488 Rules for Life*—or perhaps you've never read it, in which case, interesting choice to pick up the second book first. No judgement. Either way, I thought it might be a good idea to remind everyone that these books are a joke. It seems obvious to me, but these days disclaimers are necessary as so many people have lost their sense of humour and replaced it with a sense of outrage.

So remember, I wrote the rules to entertain you, not to enrage you. If I get it wrong occasionally or if, god forbid, I offend you, there's no need to call for my head on a spike. Just turn the page. Or do what I do when I get annoyed by a book—frisbee it across the room (preferably into a wall) then stick it in one of those street libraries full of germy books no one wants. That's not only cathartic but also a truly insidious way to leave a review and make your point without shouting or raising your blood pressure.

Unlike the original book, there are no sealed sections in this volume; however, there are special 'pandemically relevant' sections peppered throughout. These are clearly marked so you can avoid them if the very mention of Covid-19 makes you want to wade into the river with rocks in your pocket, Virginia Woolf-style. Please don't do that—simply skip the grey pages instead.

And, once again, I include a tidy reminder that none of these rules should ever be shouted at anyone. If you need to inform someone of a rule breach, let them know with a wink and a smile, maybe even a friendly shoulder chuck, 'Hey, old timer, great to see you staying active but I'm going to need you to get down from there! Rule 520 says no old men on ladders. Thanks, chief!'

Always keep it courteous and lead by example. Now let's pick up where we left off at rule number 489 . . .

THIS & THAT

LEISURE AND LIFESTYLE

489
Once a month, hold your yoga pants up to the light

If you can see through them, that means everyone else can too. And when I'm walking behind you and the sunlight hits your thinly veiled 'ass' at a certain angle, dear god, it's like I'm wearing X-ray specs. While the see-through look may have been charming and innocent in that first pic of Lady Diana outside the preschool, it's just plain confronting when it's out on the streets jiggling in front of my face. This is not fat-shaming, because I don't care how much junk you have in your trunk as long as it's covered by a generous thread count. Yoga pants should not provide a window to your soul.

490
Keep your mouth closed when applying mascara

Less of a rule and more of a challenge.

491
Don't go on about golf

Seriously, gents, you carry on as if this game is beyond the rest of us mere mortals. You also seem to think your clubs are delicate, sentient beings that need special knitted hats to keep their heads warm. I understand that the ball is small but it's also sitting completely still. In most other sports the ball moves all over the place, meaning you have to chase it down in order to catch it or hit it. If golf was really such a difficult sport, there wouldn't be so many old people playing it. The only hard thing about golf is finding the time and money you need to play it.

492
It's okay to say you don't like women playing football

Wait, don't jump on social media and cancel me, let me finish: it's okay to say you don't like women playing football, provided you don't like men playing football either. Otherwise, keep quiet.

493
Hunting is not a sport

Unless, of course, you're hunting a fellow hunter who also has a gun. Now you've got yourselves a contest.

HOUSE AND GARDEN

494
Match the size of your television to the size of your room

You actually do yourself a disservice by putting an oversized television in a regular-sized room. If you can't physically sit far enough away from the TV, your eyeballs won't be able to take in the whole screen. You'll find yourself constantly scanning left and right, up and down, in order to see everything that's happening. The exact reason none of us want to sit in the front row at the cinema. So unless you live in a stadium or you're planning to 'knock through' from your living room to the garage to create some distance, there's really no need for a billboard-sized telly.

495
No TVs above the fireplace

It's way too high. You'll do your neck. You want the centre of the screen to be roughly at eye level when you're seated. This means that only Shaquille O'Neal and a few other humans who are over seven foot tall should be mounting their TVs above the mantelpiece.

496
Think twice about a water feature

I'm all for an old-fashioned birdbath—it's a nice way to encourage the local birds to stop by for a sip of Adam's ale and a quick freshen-up. But once you start plumbing stuff in, adding a noisy

5

motor and plonking a stone buddha in the middle, it starts to feel a tad over the top, and not exactly relaxing, unless you enjoy loud, electrical, humming sounds. They're also hard work. If you don't maintain your water feature properly, you'll soon end up with a stagnant, mosquito-breeding swamp in your courtyard: 'Welcome, everyone, have you seen our Zika fountain?'

497
Buddha is not a garden gnome

Readily available in most garden centres, earthenware buddhas now sit alongside flamingos on sticks, tiki torches, miniature tin watering cans and families of gnomes. They are the hip orna-ment of choice for 'wellness' enthusiasts. And I get it, Buddha is a very relatable guy; he put on weight as he got older, his hair receded, what's not to like about him and his chilled-out teach-ings? His followers deserve a shout-out, too, for being so relaxed about Western people's penchant for sticking Buddha all over the place: in fountains and fish ponds, peering out from between the fiddle-leaf figs, perched way too close to the fire pit or barbeque. It's time to show a little more respect for the great man.

498
No armchairs in the bedroom

Unlike teenagers, who like to live, and grow mould cultures and possibly a little jazz cabbage, in their bedrooms, proper grown-ups don't spend a lot of time hanging out in their boudoir. It's really just a room for sleeping in. Which is why I find the trend for having a large comfy armchair or sofa in the bedroom rather odd. Even more odd is the fact that this chair is almost always angled to face the bed, suggesting it might be some kind of sex observation chair. By all means pop a standard chair in your room so you have something upon which to create a clothes mound instead of hanging things up, but get rid of the creepy sex-watcher armchair.

This rule is doubly important for anyone who believes in the spirit world. An armchair in the bedroom is like an open invitation for ghosts. One night you'll awaken to a familiar smack-smacking noise and look over to see the ghost of Nanna Jude sitting in the chair, sucking on a Werther's Original, waving her crochet at you.

499
Sleigh beds are for Santa and Mrs Claus

For the rest of us, they take up too much valuable real estate in the bedroom. Plus they're a pain in the arse to make every morning—reaching over, trying to tuck your sheets into the bottom end of the sleigh? Leave them for residents of the North Pole or anyone else who has elves to make the bed.

HOLIDAYS AND TRAVEL

One day the borders will reopen and we'll be able to travel again—until then, you can use this section to remind yourself of all the little things you don't miss about plane travel and holiday accommodation.

500
No irrelevant photos in the Airbnb listing

Photos of a jar of seashells in the bathroom—pointless. Same goes for that soft-focus snap of two wine glasses and a bottle of rosé on the kitchen bench. Especially if you don't plan to have said bottle of rosé sitting in the fridge for me to enjoy on arrival. Give me a close-up picture of the wi-fi password, so I know the place has internet access, a floor plan so I can see that there really are two bedrooms not just one bedroom and a cupboard with an air mattress, and maybe throw in a macro shot of the shower recess so I can check for mould. Do all that and I'll give you five stars just for your listing.

501
Provide useful amenities at your Airbnb

There appears to be some confusion over what guests actually require for an enjoyable holiday stay. Hosts seem to be under the impression that a guest's experience is enhanced by sticking giant words on the wall reminding them to DREAM, RELAX, FEEL or having decorative starfish in the bathroom to make it feel like you're under the sea when you're on the can. What guests would prefer is a sharp knife, a breadboard and a colander. Also, if it's an Airbnb, *supposedly* someone lives there, so why is the pantry completely empty? Would it kill you to have some salt and pepper in there? And if you really want to win friends and influence people, how about a little olive oil as well.

502
Two towels per person, minimum

This is not a rule; I think it's actually the law. And while we're on the topic of towels, a bath towel must be sizably bigger than a handtowel.

503
Call the council to remove hard rubbish, don't relocate it to your Airbnb

If you aren't using that hand-driven egg beater at home, there's every chance your guest won't use it either. Same goes for all those lightweight aluminium saucepans, rusty baking trays and that wonky frypan with the non-stick coating flaking off it in big black chunks.

504
White furniture is passive aggressive and unwelcoming

It says, *I dare you to sit on me.* It says, *You should expect to be charged an additional cleaning fee.* That is not, however, a free pass to go styling out your Airbnb with eye-assaulting bright-red furniture. No one can relax in a room that feels like a gaming den.

505
Respect the appliances in your hotel room

Other guests will have to use them at some stage. So don't iron black plastic bags. I can only assume this is what's happening because every time I go to use the iron in a hotel it's got black stuff melted all over it. And please don't use the kettle to boil soup.

506
Don't wear all of your luggage

Budget airlines keep the fare down by providing the bare minimum. A seat. And that's it. Anything else, like a bag or a biscuit or a bit of dignity, is going to cost you extra. That's why the canny travellers wear layer upon layer of clothing and stuff their pockets with phone chargers, shoes, iPads, bottled water, crushed up bags of McDonald's and other snacks, and then sew their jewels and valuables into the hems of their coats. Okay, maybe I made that last one up, but it's a fine line between wearing a few extra items to save on luggage costs and looking like you're escaping a fascist regime.

COMING OF AGE

A word about my generation

I am a member of Generation X, which includes anyone born between 1965 and 1980 or thereabouts. We are the generation who mistakenly believed we were going to redefine the modern world and fix everything, the ones who promised never to sell out. When Gen X poster boy Barack Obama took the reins in the United States, and a woman came to power in Australia, we thought, This is it, change starts now, time to clear up all those mistakes the Baby Boomers made. *Then, just like that (as Gen X golden girl Sarah Jessica Parker would say), we lost control. We ousted Julia Gillard from The Lodge, put a person of orange colour in charge of the White House and handed everything back to the conservative white men. What happened? Did we get lazy? Greedy? Did we become obsessed with stuff like home ownership and naming our kids after poets? Did we sell out? Did I just start writing like Carrie Bradshaw?*

I have separate rules for each generation, but I will start with Gen X. Not because I'm angry with us—I'm not—I'm just really, really disappointed.

GENERATION X

507
Accept that you have been rubbed down with vanishing cream

Lacking the wealth of the Baby Boomers and the youth of the Millennials, Generation X is currently the forgotten generation. Millennials, for example, don't even acknowledge that we exist as a separate demographic; they simply refer to anyone over forty as a 'Boomer'. Fair enough. We have been getting increasingly conservative about stuff. On the bright side, the Baby Boomers can't last forever and when they become extinct, hopefully it will be Gen X who inherit all that sweet, sweet Baby Boomer real estate. And then Millennials will *have* to acknowledge us, specifically for the purpose of hating us.

508
Not every band needs to get back together

By all means dust off those instruments and muck around in the garage or the backyard and talk about the good old days with your buds. But think very carefully before you drag your asses back onto a public stage and start charging your friends money to attend your reunion 'concert'. Respect that they might find it tough to watch your middle-aged paunch straining at those shirt buttons as you 'rock out' and sweat profusely under the hot lights. A sweaty young man on stage is one thing, but a sweaty fifty-something just makes everyone nervous and wonder if the venue has a defibrillator.

509
The time for giant underpants is now

Stop clinging to the vestiges of your come-hither youth and make the switch to big undies. The bigger the better. You want something comfortable enough to sit around in all day. You want to enjoy the secure feeling of pants that pull all the way up to your under-bosom. Forget about visible panty lines—your knickers will be riding so high everyone is going to mistake your VPL for a bra strap. Big underpants are like Jesus: you need to accept them into your life and wear them up close to your heart.

510
Don't use the phrase 'Okay Boomer'

This rejoinder is not for you, Gen X, it belongs to the youth. They came up with it, they're the ones who get to use it to dismiss anyone a minute older than them. Credit where it's due, it's a pretty good shutdown. Sure, it's overused and technic-ally inaccurate when they use it to scoff at Gen Xers. However, I will maintain my dignity and not get upset about that. There's nothing sadder than being 'okay boomered' and then desperately protesting 'But I'm Generation X!' All the young person hears is yet another old person making complaining noises.

Oh and also, 'nek minnit' finished a while back. You shouldn't say that either.

511
Leave the kooky glasses for Sir Elton

If you find your hand hovering above the oversized, coloured, 'statement' frames in the spectacle shop, remind yourself it's a slippery slope. You're only middle-aged at the moment, do you really want to fast-track yourself to old age? Because one minute you're putting big fun glasses on your face, the next you're heading out with bandaids on your face. Careful.

512
Put down the iPad stylus

I'm sure it works a treat but you look silly—like a four year old scrabbling away on a Magna Doodle, or the South Koreans in 2010 when they were using cocktail sausages to stab at their iPhones because their fingers wouldn't work in the cold weather. Come on, Gen X, don't be giving up on your body parts just yet; the time will come when you can sit around complaining about how things ache and don't work anymore but until then, no styluses.

513
Beware the unreliable sphincter

At some point during your late forties, your FWS (fart warning system) starts taking the occasional micro-nap. The majority of the time, you're totally in control; you sense trouble brewing below and you have time to either move away and release in a safe space, or clench and store it up for later. Sometimes, however, as you age, you get caught off guard. Your FWS goes down, and the first you know about it is when that pent-up air fires out of you like a gunshot and reverberates around the room or, indeed, Spotlight (if you're unlucky like me). The trick is knowing how to react when a surprise fart attack occurs. The best thing to do is to stand perfectly still. You need to freeze in position and catch the eye of someone nearby. Affect a look of mild disdain and raise an eyebrow at them. With any luck you'll have them thinking, *Oh my god, was that me?*

514
Don't trust 'facts' about vaccines that you find on Facebook

Of all the demographics, Gen X has fallen the hardest for Facebook, and it shows. Once we were the cool, 'we invented Nirvana and The Big Day Out' generation; now we're the vax-hesitant, 'I don't trust the science because I read something alarmist on Facebook' generation. Scientists and medical researchers do all the heavy lifting and experimenting so we don't have to. It seems the only mistake they make is publishing their findings in peer-reviewed journals rather than posting them on Facebook. Time to give real science a few more likes.

BABY BOOMERS

515
Start every story with 'Stop me if I've told you this already'

As an old person, you have lived a long life and no doubt have plenty of stories, so why not dig deep and roll out some new content occasionally? We're all happy to let you have the talking stick, we just want to hear something different.

516
You must be in the same room to converse

You cannot shout at someone who is in a different part of the house and expect them to hear you. Would somebody please tell my parents.

517
Let the young person operate the iPad

If you want to show a young person something on your iPad, hand it over and let them drive it. It's hard for the tech-savvy youth to watch Baby Boomers tapping all over the screen, swiping up and down with an absurd and unnecessary level of vigour. I swear my mother gets a full upper-body workout every time she uses her iPad. Shoulder reconstructions are going to be the new knee replacements if old people don't take the swiping down a notch.

518
Resist the urge to share your ancestry.com research

This is not to suggest you shouldn't enjoy a good old rummage through your family history. If you've got the time, why not get on that iPad you love so much and start searching through the past. Just be aware that no one, not even members of your own family, will be as interested in your findings as you are. Unless, of course, your ancestor was some kind of eighteenth-century 'pants man' who dipped his wick all over the village and eventually died of syphilis. Nothing captures an audience's attention like syphilis.

519
Don't be afraid to embellish your findings

If you must share your family history, then get creative with it. True doesn't always equate to interesting, and you should never let the facts get in the way of some good ancestry. I guarantee the program *Who Do You Think You Are?* embellishes all the time. No one would watch it if they kept 'uncovering' pedestrian things like Russell Crowe's great-great-aunt was a seamstress. Boo. I'm bored. I want to hear that his great-great-aunt lived as a man, Albert Nobbs–style, and went on to become a world champion bare-knuckle boxer (who eventually died of syphilis).

520
Men's ladder privileges expire at fifty-five

Unless you're a tradie, in which case, I'll spot you a few extra years. But for the rest of you, get down from there. Seriously fellas, it's not going to end well.

521
Don't take photos with your iPad

Nothing gives away your age faster than holding up a giant tablet in front of your face to take a picture. I'm well aware that your iPad has a camera, but just because you *can* take photos with it, doesn't mean you should.

522
Just,, checkyr TEXT before))) you spend it clapping hands, screaming face emoji

Baby Boomers still seem largely unaware of predictive text and the role it can play in rendering your texts indecipherable. You need to check that all the words make sense, watch out for random punctuation and review any emojis to make sure they're conveying the right emojion. It's weird to get a crying laughing face at the end of a text that says 'We had to take the dog to the vet.' Possibly you've got a bad case of 'fat finger' combined with 'can't find my glasses' and you keep hitting the wrong things by accident. Or maybe it's time to consider getting a stylus. Oh I'm kidding! Just proofread your work before you press send.

523
Don't send memes to Millennials

They saw it two years ago. Gen X, this goes for you too. Don't send memes to your Gen Z kids. The basic rule of thumb is that memes can be traded *up* to the generation above or *within* your own generation. Don't meme down.

524
Get to the good bit

As people get older, they begin to obsess over the really unimportant details of a story. Like what time it was and what day of the week it happened. 'So, Jean was at the golf club on Monday. Hang on ... was it Monday? No ... I don't think it was Monday, maybe it was Tuesday ... Actually, do you know what? I think it was Wednesday.' Oh for god's sake, you're not Craig David, it doesn't matter what day it happened. Get to the bit about Jean being struck by lightning as she teed off!

MILLENNIALS

I feel it's pointless laying down rules for Millennials. They'll just 'Okay Boomer' anything written here. But sometimes it can be cathartic to shout into the wind, so here goes.

525
Learn to cook

Signing up for Hello Fresh or Marley's Spoon or Bitch Be Cookin' Din Dins isn't really cooking. Stop kidding yourself, you're not *that* busy. Put a podcast on and make some pasta.

526
Turn up for work unless you're sick

A lot of Millennials don't seem to realise that if you want to take a day off work, you need to be sick—or at least pretending to be sick. Instead, they believe you have the right to skip work anytime it's inconvenient.

I know a Millennial who texted their boss to say they couldn't come in because the fence had fallen down and they were worried about their dog escaping. As a devoted dog owner who would never put my dogs' welfare at risk, I completely understand this dilemma. As a person who knows the rules, however, I can tell you there are countless solutions to this problem.

You could put the dog in the house and go to work.

If you don't trust the dog in the house, put the dog in the laundry and go to work. If you don't have a laundry, stick the dog in the bathroom and go to work. You could take the dog to a friend's house and go to work. Take the dog to your mum's house and go to work.

As I said, there are myriad solutions to this problem and pretty much all of them end with 'and go to work'.

527
If you do call in 'sick', stay off social media

Too sick to work? Then you're too sick to go to the beach. I'm not saying you can't go to the beach, I'm saying don't be foolish enough to post pictures of yourself at the beach. Show a modicum of intelligence.

528
Forget the eighties

If there is a decade of fashion that should be consigned to the rubbish bin rather than the recycling, it's the eighties. When you look back at movies from the sixties you think, *Ooh gee, don't they all look tidy!* Even looking back at the seventies you can still find plenty of positives: certain men really rocked those hip-hugging tight pants and large lapels, as did some ladies. However, eighties fashion did nothing for no one. No one was rocking it.

Take a movie like *Working Girl* from 1988, for example. Melanie Griffith played an ambitious young secretary keen to be taken seriously as a businesswoman, yet she was dressed like a portly Amish woman with shoulder pads?

That's what eighties fashion did, it made everyone look like stout middle-aged women. And there's absolutely nothing wrong with looking like a stout middle-aged woman, provided you are one. But we were teenagers and twenty-somethings. So could Millennials please stop trying to bring back this vile decade by referring to it as 'vintage'? It's very triggering. And you look dreadful, just like we did. You'll be sorry.

GENERATION Z

There's a lot to love about Generation Z. I love their faces, unravaged by time or surgery. I love that they decided to protest climate change by taking the day off school. What a simple and yet ingenious way to get more young people to turn up and support the cause. And may I say, you're going to need a lot more of that ingenuity if you're ever going to fix this mess of a planet we've gifted you. So Generation Z, I wish you all the best; here are a few rules I hope might be of help.

529
TikTok is not a job

It's been a tough time for Gen Z. Thanks to the pandemic, you've missed a lot of seminal moments in your school or university years. Graduations, formals, schoolies—they all got cancelled, but that doesn't mean you can't still aspire to greatness or at least do a little more with your life than make TikTok videos. Also, that platform is creepy; you do realise it actually spies on you and observes your expressions? TikTok is the modern-day equivalent of the dirty old perv hiding in the bushes watching you.

530
Don't eat your meals in the bedroom

The bedroom is for sleeping and, if you must, gaming. The kitchen and dining room are the eating chambers of the house and you should avail yourselves of these wonderful amenities. Don't hibernate in your bedroom surrounded by towers of dirty bowls and cups. Both you and the room need some fresh air, air that isn't heavy with the stench of your latest Uber Eats delivery. Parents need to play their part in this rule too—if you want to lure the kids out of their burrows, you need to promise not to badger them with questions like 'Did you only just wake up?!' or 'Aren't you supposed to go to work today?' or 'Have you filled out that form yet?' or 'How many people will be at the party?'

531
Be patient with old people who get your pronoun wrong

We're working on it, I promise.

532
Not everything is a toxic message

Sometimes your parents just say dumb stuff. So do you. Cut each other some slack.

533
Anyone sleeping over needs to come out and say hello

You are the generation that is in no rush to move out of home and who can blame you? Rent is expensive and house prices are laughable. Plus you have Gen X parents who are desperate to be seen as the 'cool parents'. They're not just Mum and Dad, they're your pal, your BFF, your bestie. And that is really working in your favour. Many teens now get given a double bed. Not only that, a lot of you are allowed to have sex in your bedroom. Some of the sensible/I'm-too-young-to-be-a-grandparent parents even put condoms in your drawers. It's a pretty sweet deal and nothing like the old days when teens had to clamber in and out of bedroom windows to avoid getting caught together. You need to show your appreciation for all these perks by offering your parents a crumb of congeniality in return. Whoever sleeps over in your bedroom must come out and say hello in the morning. It's potentially awkward, sure, but just tell your friend to pop some pants on (please) and come out to say hi. Trust me, it will make your parents' day.

534
Be discreet

During your 'sleepovers', keep the noise down. No sounds of enjoyment should escape the walls. That's the small price you pay for being allowed to do it at home. You must do it quietly. 'Cos you know what's even more awkward and uncomfortable than the thought of your parents 'doing it'? The thought of your kids doing it.

SPECIAL PANDEMIC TIMES SECTION
THE BASICS

In the beginning we tried to be positive. We waxed on about getting to know our neighbours (mostly because we were desperate to talk to anyone who didn't live inside our own four walls) and we hashtag glad-gamed about the lack of traffic on the roads and not having to do the daily commute. Working mothers revelled in a sense of schadenfreude as they listened to men complain about how hard it is to work from home with the kids running around. And we turned every day into Christmas Day, selflessly keeping Australia Post afloat as Postman Santa worked around the clock to deliver all those late-night, wine-fuelled

online purchases we made with PayPal (or as I like to call it, 'pretend click money').

I tried to take comfort in the little things, like getting to see how messy other people's houses were, courtesy of Zoom. I'd always assumed my pigsty of a home was the outlier, but it turns out loads of people are untidy. It made me feel good, but also made me wonder why these people didn't do what I do and keep one small corner of the house tidy for Zoom meetings.

In the beginning, I never imagined I'd need to write a bunch of rules for a pandemic but now, almost two years into this thing, with everyone thinking, 'Jesus Christ, when will it END?!' I see that I have no choice. It's time to pivot and apply my special rule-making gift to this global crisis.

535
Stop chowing down on endangered species

Whether you believe Covid-19 started in a bat, a lab, Bill Gates' secret lair or a weird scaly animal at a wet market in Wuhan, this rule shouldn't be exclusive to pandemic times. Note, please: I am not having a stab at China here—I have no beef with China. Nor do many of our cattle producers at the moment, apparently. I'm just suggesting we could all lay off eating exotic and endangered species. Especially if the only reason you're doing it is because you think their ground-up horns or toenails will give you a magical erection. I know it's hard to believe but some things are slightly more important than your penis, guys.

536
Don't hoard like an idiot

Not once, in any state, at any time, have the supermarkets closed. There has never been an actual shortage of anything. The only reason anyone has been forced to go without pasta or mince or toilet paper is because panic buyers stripped the shelves. I imagine doomsday preppers around the world watched footage of those frenzied supermarket shoppers in disbelief. Preppers know better than to run blindly into a store and start grabbing mindlessly at whatever's in front of them. (They also know that once a lockdown has been called, it's too late, you've missed the boat.) So if you really must hoard, do it like a pro: hoard hard and hoard early. Obviously you want to avoid anything that needs refrigeration 'cos you don't want to drain your 'genny' (that's prepper talk for generator). You need to grab packet soups, Spam, canned fish or cat food (it's the same thing), powdered milk and, I would also suggest, some sheets of nori. Seaweed contains a lot of essential vitamins and minerals and could potentially double as toilet paper in an emergency.

537
No fighting in the supermarket aisles

Given that there will always be people who ignore the no-hoarding rule, it's up to the rest of us to lead by example. Walk away from a shouting match or physical scrap in the supermarket. Reassure yourself that, as a species, humans have survived for hundreds of thousands of years. We're bipedal cockroaches. Look at North Korea: they haven't had food for decades, and while you might not fancy a bowl of stick and gravel soup, it does seem to be sustaining a large percentage of the North Korean population.

As for brawling over toilet paper, have you lost your mind, man? Maintain your dignity, use your oversized human brain and come up with a solution. How about washing your bumhole? Lots of men out there for whom that wouldn't be a bad idea, toilet paper shortage or not. Sluicing out your bot might be slightly inconvenient but I'm making the point that there is always an alternative to punching on with someone in Woolworths. After all, it's only a pandemic, not the zombie apocalypse.*

* *FYI, when the zombies come, all bets are off. I'm shooting you in the head and prising the toilet paper out of your cold dead hands.*

538
Dance like nobody's watching, shop like somebody's filming

If you think you might struggle to remember the rule about not fighting in supermarkets, then perhaps this will help you keep yourself nice—always assume that someone, somewhere is filming you, which means the minute you do anything stupid you will be publicly shamed by every news outlet around the world. None of the networks care anymore about broadcast quality. They'll take out-of-focus, jerky iPhone footage any day, provided it shows members of the public screaming and beating one another with value packs of pasta.

539
Support your local bakery

The bakery is considered an essential service. It's open. I know you've been on the internet and learnt how to make sourdough. I know your loaf was made with love (tonnes of it, if the weight of the loaf is anything to go by) and I know everyone in the house took turns feeding 'the mother'. Together you created a loaf that made you feel more connected as a family. And I'm sure that with half a pound of butter slathered on every slice, that loaf is perfectly edible. You had a go and good on you, but that's enough now. It's time to admit that lockdowns are hard enough and you shouldn't punish yourself with dense bricks of damp dough. Get some properly delicious bread from the bakery.

540
Before you 'pivot' your business to produce hand sanitiser, make sure you have a decent recipe

After living with Covid-19 for this long, many of us are now hand-sanitiser connoisseurs. In the beginning we really appreciated the many small businesses who stepped up to help meet demand and manufacture much-needed hand sanitiser. But with supply now well under control, it feels like a good time to finesse your formula if you plan to stay in the sanitiser game. You're aiming for something that doesn't sting like pure alcohol, doesn't smell like paint stripper or a trough lolly, and doesn't run all over your hands like water. Oh, and thank you for your service.

541
Don't make a TV show about life in lockdown

No one wants to watch that. If you're going to spend money on TV production, make something that helps us forget about the pandemic. We've got the news if we want to be depressed.

542
Scan the QR code and step aside to fill out the rest

And, yes, I'm afraid I'm looking at you, old people. God bless you for checking in, just please be aware of the pile-up happening behind you.

SHOP TALK

CONSUMERS

543
No one needs special cheese cutlery

Cheese is fairly easy to cut, as evidenced by the late-night infomercials that advertise items like the 'Miracle Knife' or the 'Wonder Blade'. They never use a wheel of cheese in these demonstrations. The shouty presenter is always carving through things like tin cans and old leather shoes. But a chunk o' cheddar? Nup. Because *any* knife will cut cheese. In fact, I'm pretty confident any spoon will cut cheese. I've even used a wooden chopstick to cut cheese; it's not ideal but it works fine. My point is, your kitchen drawer overfloweth with cheese-cutting implements, you do not need to buy a special miniature cheese cleaver. Unless, of course, you are a mouse and you have some serial killing to do.

544
Always buy a backup avocado

The avocado is a high-risk purchase, so if your meal is avocado-dependent you don't want to bet the house on one single fruit. And if you're a straight man who has been sent to get the groceries, I suggest you buy at least three.

545
Avoid single-use appliances

Much like specific cutlery for cheese, there are plenty of items you and your kitchen can live without. Even if you have room in your 'butler's pantry', why not save the space, save your money and invest in an actual butler to live in there instead. I guarantee you already have everything you need in your kitchen to prepare delicious food. Show me your rice cooker, I will show you my saucepan with a well-fitting lid; show me your milkshake-maker, I will show you my blender; show me your elaborate countertop coffee-maker, I will show you my beardy guy with the man bun down at the local cafe.

But, just in case you've been watching too many cooking shows and are feeling tempted, here is a detailed list of things you don't need.

SOUS VIDE MACHINE

I'm not a French speaker but I believe *sous vide* translates to 'over-rated slow-boiled meat' and the good news is, you don't need a special machine to make that magic happen. Just pop your steak into a ziplock bag, boil for forty minutes and voila! You're halfway to that classic French bistro dish, Warm Grey Meat & Frites. Enjoy.

FOOD DEHYDRATOR

Don't be tempted by this contraption, mostly because if you look around your kitchen you'll see you already have one. It's called an oven. Stick it on low and start drying out all the food you need for that trip to space you must be planning. Why else would you be dehydrating food?

AIRFRYER

Due to its size, the airfryer is often mistaken for a small caravan, and you might actually find yourself needing to park it out on the street for the 364 days of the year you're not using it. The enjoyable paradox of this huge appliance is its relatively tiny cooking basket, which holds a mere handful of chips. If you're that worried about cooking with too much oil, try putting less oil on your food before cooking it.

ICE CREAM MAKER

You really don't have to make everything 'from scratch'. Modern life is not a self-sufficiency competition and there's no actual survivalist value in making your own ice cream. Plant a few herbs instead.

EGG POACHER

None of them work. None. If you need a foolproof way to poach an egg, I refer you to season one, episode one, of the program *Amy Schumer Learns to Cook*. Even my nephew has mastered this method to perfectly poach eggs for himself every morning.

RETAILERS

546
Don't misdirect the buying public

Recently I sat myself down in a very swanky-looking cocktail bar and looked up at the unfamiliar list of cocktails on the wall, things like Buzz Cut, Hot Towel Shave and Lemon Myrtle Pomade. Fortunately I realised I was in a barber shop before I ordered a delicious sounding Tidy Beard Sculpt. Given the huge hit retail has taken during the pandemic, now seems like a good time to remind vendors of the need to be clear about the goods and services on offer. Besides the barber shop/wine bar confusion, I've noticed that many real estate agencies are now fitting themselves out like cafes. I've also mistaken the post office for a two-dollar shop, Aldi for a rubbish tip and a tattoo parlour for a jewellery store (that necklace is never coming off).

547
Put the cash registers at the front, Kmart

Kmart moved their registers to the middle of the store, claiming it was to keep the entrances clear and allow for easy coming and going. But shoppers aren't stupid. We know why they did it. For the same reason supermarkets put the milk at the back of the store—so that you're forced to walk past umpteen other tempting items on the way. Kmart think they have created a fun treasure-hunt experience. Their hope is that as you search for the tills 'buried' in the middle of the store, you will pass loads of other precious treasure and be tempted to add it to your cart. But the problem is, Kmart, you don't sell treasure, you sell landfill.

548
Not everything needs to be 'monetised'

It's okay to keep your hobby as something you enjoy doing in your free time. Don't feel pressured by overly supportive friends and family who say things like, 'Oh my god, these pupcakes are amazing, my dog loves them, you should totally go on Shark Tank, you could make a fortune.' You could . . . but you probably won't and there's every chance you'll stop enjoying making marrow muffins for mutts once you have to worry about spreadsheets and inventory and distribution and all those other boring business things. Also, let's be honest, not everything needs to be scaled up. Some things were meant to be sold only at markets. Things like jewellery made from forks, hemp-based baby swaddles, flavoured honey that never tastes any different to regular honey, tree-stump furniture and upcycled shopping bag aprons. And if you're a scented candlemaker, you definitely want to keep that small-scale and recreational. The market is awash with scented candles, so much so that if the global wax mines dried up tomorrow, we would still have enough candles for everyone, forever.

CAFES

549
Remove the lettuce before toasting the sandwich

I understand it's fast and convenient to have your sandwiches prepped and waiting in the glass cabinet and that it's inconvenient to take the lettuce off, then toast the sandwich, then put the lettuce back on, but no one wants a chicken and hot lettuce sandwich. Full disclosure, my mother asked me to include this rule.

550
Baristas must be able to talk and froth simultaneously

No one minds a chatty barista, provided they are able to talk and make the coffee at the same time. But when you are standing at the back of a long line and the barista keeps taking his foot off the frothing gas in order to chitty chat, that's when the customers start getting antsy. Talk and froth, guys, talk and froth.

551
Three takeaway coffees max per customer

During peak periods, cafes should be allowed to put up a sign that limits customers to two or three takeaway coffees. We've all been on a tight schedule, walked past the cafe, seen a couple of people queuing and thought, *Yep, I've got time, I'll make it* and joined the end of the line. Only to have some clown in front of you get to the counter and start rattling off a coffee order for the entire office, punctuating said order with, 'Oh and do you do milkshakes by any chance?'

552
Social distance your diners

This is not about venue capacity during a pandemic; this pertains to those waiters who insist on seating you right on top of other diners when there are still plenty of free tables elsewhere in the restaurant. The oft-volunteered excuse of 'I'm sorry, I have to sit you in my section' is baloney. If there is genuinely such a strict demarcation of sections, then sit me in someone else's section and send that section-master over to take my order. Or, if there's no one on shift yet to service that section, make like a politician and cross the floor yourself.

553
Put some thought into the vegetarian option

Vegetarians appreciate it when you have an option for them; they are not ungracious people. But there is not a vegetarian in the world who needs to eat another stuffed mushroom, stuffed capsicum, or anything that relies on huge chunks of cold, wet pumpkin. And for the love of god, stop calling slabs of vegetables set into a solid block of egg a 'fritatta'—that's not a fritatta, it's an 'egg-wodge' and no one likes it.

554
No naked leaves

Putting a bunch of dry greenery on the side of a plate is tantamount to food waste. You may as well throw it straight in the bin. But if you toss those leaves in a decent amount of dressing, then we'll have a go at them.

555
Hang up before you approach the counter

All shops and cafes should be allowed to have a sign on the door that clearly states:

FOR HEALTH AND SAFETY REASONS,
WE CANNOT SERVE YOU WHILE YOU ARE ON THE PHONE

Because when you walk in yammering away on your phone, pause momentarily to bark out a coffee order then go right back to your call, it takes a lot of restraint for the person behind the counter not to reach out, snatch that phone and whack you over the head with it. So, for your own safety, please get off the phone and engage in a courteous and human-like manner with the shopkeep. And don't excuse yourself by saying that the call is important. if it was that important, you wouldn't be stopping to get a coffee.

CLEAR COMMUNICATION

TEXTING AND EMAILING

556
No one really believes 'OMG! I just saw this msg now for some reason!'

It's like when someone doesn't reply to your email for weeks then sends a missive headed 'OMG I just found your email in my junk folder.' Maybe that's true, or maybe you're a liar liar, pants on fire, in which case it's much better to start your text or email with a simple 'Sorry I've taken so long to reply.' No need to elaborate, just offer an apology, straight up with no qualifier. The exception to this rule is if the email saying 'I just found this in my junk folder' comes from me, in which case I swear it's true.

557
Abbreviations in texts should be easy to decipher

Occasionally you have to concede that sending a WTF or an OMG is convenient—it may not be your personal style, but everyone understands the impulse to send them. Other abbreviations, however, will simply never catch on. When has 'tks' ever saved anyone time? It's not immediately obvious it means 'thanks', so all it does is momentarily confuse the reader. It really would be quicker to just tap out the word 'thanks'; it's not a long word and I'll tk you not to waste my time in future.

558
Don't avoid the grieving

As a general rule, it's perfectly fine to send a tasteful text when someone dies. Not to the dead person (obviously) but to the family and friends. Don't hand-wring over the idea that you might 'interrupt the grieving process' or that you didn't know the family well enough to send a text. And definitely don't *not* send a text because you're worried about saying the wrong thing. All of these things are about you. People like to know you're thinking about them, so text them and let them know, just don't expect a reply; recognise that the grief text is a one-way exchange.

Important caveat for anyone over sixty—when signing off on a text to a grieving person, remember LOL does not stand for lots of love.

559
e-cards are meaningless

They say either, 'I forgot' or 'I didn't care enough to get you an actual card but I still want the points for sending one'. I would much rather you just sent me a three-word email that said, 'Happy birthday, mate!' Or one of those text messages that does something explosive when you open it up: fireworks go off, balloons float up, confetti rains down or, the best one, lasers crisscross the screen—that one actually makes noise and buzzes in your hand. It's a multi-sensory experience. I get such a childish kick out of receiving them, I often play them over and over. If you don't know what I'm talking about, ask a young person to send you one; they're quite magical.

560
Don't weaponise your birthday

After a certain age, it really doesn't matter if people forget your birthday. Everyone's busy. And no one is forgetting your birthday to spite you. One of my mother's main jobs in our family is to text everyone else a reminder that someone's birthday is coming up so no one feels forgotten. This year I decided to cut out the middle man and send the reminder to my siblings myself. As soon as I woke up, I texted, 'Hi guys, it's my birthday today, don't forget to send me a text saying *Happy Birthday*.' It was a big success. We've agreed this is the way forward.

KIDS PARTY INVITATIONS

561
Be specific, leave nothing open to interpretation

In days of yore (well, back in the seventies) my mother used to drop me at my friends' birthday parties by slowing the car down, shouting, 'Tuck and roll!' then pushing me out the door. I'd barely be through the front gate before she was out of sight and already enjoying her child-free afternoon.

Not so these days. Parents tend to stick around. So not only do you have to entertain the kids, you also have to entertain the parents. Which can be a lot of work, especially if you don't really know these parents. I understand that when kids are very young, you might want other parents to stay and help wrangle a house full of preschoolers hopped up on sugar and party vibes. But once the kids can competently toilet themselves and articulate things like 'Joshua has fallen off the trampoline and now his leg looks weird', lingering parents can be a real drag. To avoid any confusion, I suggest making it clear on the invitation, much like you would with a dress code. Simply state: 'This is a Drop & Go event. Drop at 2 pm. Go. Pick up at 5 pm.' Do not, under any circumstances, forget to state the pick-up time.

LANGUAGE

I understand English is a living language but that doesn't mean we shouldn't be able to kill things off occasionally.

562
You can't verse people

You can play against or versus a person. But to say 'I'm versing someone' sounds as if you're aggressively reciting poetry at them.

563
Medal is not a verb

It's time to return to 'winning medals' at the Olympics rather than 'medalling'. Medalling makes it sound like you're talking about a pesky kid who snuck into the athletes' village and mixed up the urine samples. Plus, we all know that if an athlete has medalled it's just code for 'didn't win gold'. Same goes for podium. No one is podiuming. Or has podiumed. Or will be podiuming. Can you not hear how ridiculous it sounds?

564
Talk 'about it' not 'to it'

This recent affectation of speaking 'to' things rather than about things has really taken off.

'Hmm, you raise an interesting point about language, can you speak *to* that some more?'

I can only assume people think it makes them sound intellectual when, in reality, it makes them sound like someone who's watched too many Oprah interviews.

565
Stop devaluing words

'Absolutely' is used so often in place of the word 'yes' that it has little meaning anymore as a word that adds emphasis. Youthful call centre operators also like to abuse adjectives such as 'amazing' and 'fantastic', using them to punctuate the most pedestrian exchanges:

'Can I start with your name?'

'Sam.'

'Amazing. And is this the phone number you're calling about?'

'Yep.'

'Faaantastic.'

Hmm, is it? I would argue that being able to cite things like your own name, address and phone number is completely unremarkable unless you're recovering from some kind of *Memento*-style traumatic memory loss.

Similarly, we've managed to wreck the words 'awesome' and 'epic'. They both now mean little more than 'okay'.

'I'll pick up some cat food on my way home.'

'Awesome, that would be epic.'

Hardly. Even my cat, who loves food more than life itself, would tell you that response is disproportionate. At best it deserves a thumbs up and a thankyou.

566
Optics schmoptics

This is really the same as the above, with people thinking they sound more intelligent if they say 'The optics aren't good on that' rather than 'Ooh gee, that looks bad'. And while we're at it, referring to a lamp as 'a piece' and the room as 'the space' just makes you sound up yourself.

567
Four things you shouldn't say about yourself

I'm a smart person.
I'm very creative.
I'm really good in bed.
I'm such an empath.

Rest assured it's okay to *think* all of these things about yourself, and it's perfectly fine for other people to say these things about you. But when you say them yourself, unfortunately all anyone hears is 'I'm a bit of a dick.'

568
Four things you shouldn't say to try to sound interesting

I'm a clean freak.
I'm thinking about quitting sugar.
I'm a full-on foodie.
I'm passionate about event management.

Again, there is nothing wrong with doing or being any of these things, just don't mistake them for conversation starters.

569
Four things you shouldn't ask a teenager

What subjects are you doing?
Who was at the party?
Why don't you open the blinds?
Is there a funny smell in here?

570
Don't use the word 'hubby'

I know it's quick and easy but for some reason 'hubby' always conjures up an image of a chubby man hiding in a cupboard, rather than the grown man who is your husband.

571
Curb your Americanisms

I don't mind the occasional Americanism—for example, anaesthesiologist looks hard but is actually easier to say than anaesthetist. Others, however, are just plain grating, especially when they come out of children's mouths. I think teachers should put up posters around our classrooms to remind kids that in this country we say:

Bum not butt
Poo not poop
Lollies not candy
My fault not my bad

And as for 'dang it'—why are we letting Australian kids talk like hillbillies? I think I'd almost prefer they said 'f**k it'. Almost. Cookie vs biscuit is mildly controversial. I acknowledge that biscuit is what we say here in Australia; however, I will accept cookie when preceded by 'homemade chocolate chip' or indeed 'Oreo'. Conversely, Anzac can only be followed by biscuit. In fact, I believe that saying 'Anzac cookie' could see you arrested for treason.

572
Ass is funny, arse is harsh

Many readers might have expected ass and arse to be included in the rule about curbing Americanisms. However, this is a tricky one for me. I often use 'ass' in my writing because I think it sounds amusing. And, in my mind, ass is also less aggressive than arse. 'Move your fat ass.' That's funny. 'Move your fat arse.' You just crossed a line, that's highly offensive. But here's the twist: I would never call someone an 'asshole'—it feels weak and ineffectual. If you're annoyed with someone to the point of insulting them, then you want a word with a bit of punch. And that's arsehole. Always arsehole. It's a good, strong word. Basically, what I've just admitted is that all my rules are completely arbitrary, subjective nonsense. Enjoy.

SPECIAL PANDEMIC TIMES SECTION
MASKS

Trigger warning:
Please skip the next few pages if the idea of
wearing a mask makes you apoplectic and inclined
to send me death threats. I'm here to entertain,
not to enrage. You've been warned, so either move
on or climb aboard my mask-wearing train!

573
Wear a mask

I'm a big believer in science and this one's been proven time and time again by an experiment that even I can understand. It's quite literally, 'Okay everyone, look how far spit droplets go *without* a mask on. Now look how far they go *with* a mask on.' Try it at home if you don't believe me. First spit with a mask off, then spit again with a mask on. The results will amaze you.

574
Brush your teeth before putting your mask on

One of the worst things about wearing a mask is being confronted with the occasional reality of your own bad breath. Brushing before fitting your mask can stop you going into a daily spiral of 'Oh my god, is this acrid stench what I've been breathing on people my entire life? How do I still have any friends?' You might want to carry mints for when brushing is not an option but avoid extra-strong mints if you wear glasses, 'cos the fumes that get funnelled up from those suckers are enough to melt your eyeballs.

575
Masks go over mouths and noses

People who wear their mask at half-mast with their nose hanging out over the top don't seem to understand the function of the mask, or indeed the nose. The mask is there to stop droplets and germs; the nose is there to help you breathe and produce snot. In other words, the core business of the nose is to make and dispense droplets and germs. I don't think anyone should be fined for incorrect mask wearing, instead I think they should be forced to wear an exemption in the form of a T-shirt that says I'M A MOUTH-BREATHER.

576
Don't feel obliged to have fun with masks

A standard paper mask is fine. It's enough that you wear a mask and tolerate it, no one expects you to enjoy it or make it a fun fashion statement.

577
Focus on the positives

In summer, wearing a mask can be stifling, but in winter it does quite a nice job of keeping your face warm, kind of like a balaclava without the terrorist overtones. Masks also make close-talkers and people with bad breath a lot more bearable. As for bank robbers? Why on earth aren't they all out robbing themselves stupid? Gone are the signs that say, *Remove your face covering before entering the bank*. These days you're not allowed in the bank *without* covering your face. So stop sitting around complaining about the restrictions and get out there, you clowns, it's salad days for bank robbers! (Just be aware that depending on lockdown laws, you might need to restrict your robbing to within a five to ten kilometre radius of your hideout.)

578
Don't argue with retail staff about
your right not to wear a mask

Take it up with the government. Or take it to the streets and protest about your right to spread Covid, whatever you need to do in order to 'feel heard'. And if you're running out of ways to demonstrate that the rules don't apply to you—if punching horses and setting off flares in the CBD isn't sending your message strongly enough—then might I suggest you start burning my books? I'd be so touched, and I really think it would make your point about not believing in rules.

Just don't be a coward and make your stand by shouting at some poor person in a shop or a cafe, someone who neither makes the rules nor has any power to change the rules. Anti-maskers love to bellow about rights but what about the rights of the person behind the counter? Surely they have the right not to be abused in their own workplace?

579
Show your exemption letter politely

I know some people have legitimate grounds for not wearing a mask and it must get boring being asked to show your exemption letter all the time, but hey, it's boring for a fisherman to be asked if they're 'catching any today' or a cab driver to be asked 'You just starting or finishing?' or breakfast radio presenters to be asked 'What time do you have to get up in the morning?' But they all still manage to respond politely. Waving your exemption aggressively in somebody's face makes it difficult to read and also creates suspicion. Hang on, is that a genuine exemption you're flapping or is it just something you printed off the web? Something that says, 'I am a sovereign citizen, I have the right not to wear a mask according to subsection (b) of law 251 of Internet-Land.'

FOOD STUFF

EATING

580
Never make eye contact with someone while eating a banana

After about the age of twelve, you need to be mindful of your banana consumption. What was once a fun fruit for monkeys and children suddenly becomes an undignified, innuendo-laden snack. Eat them in public if you must but keep your eyes cast downwards.

581
No eating on the phone

Be aware that people usually take a phone call by holding the phone to their ear. So if you're chewing while talking to someone on the phone, the sound of your smack-smackery is going directly into their earhole. It's like you've put your mouth right onto their ear and started masticating. It's offensive.

582
Bring your food up to your mouth, don't take your face down to your plate

Food is always exciting when it arrives at the table but it's important to remember, we're not livestock in a barn. Keep your head up, don't lower it down to the trough and start snuffling.

583
If your food is too hot, stop eating it

We've all seen idiots do it. And we've all been the idiot who's done it, whether it's tucking into a bowl of visibly steaming risotto or a pizza straight out of the oven covered in molten lava-like cheese. You take a bite and instantly know you've made a mistake. You wave your hand up and down in front of your open mouth, fanning the food and huffing out words of warning to everyone at the table: 'Ahhh, haht, haht, haht, 's too haht!' Then you start chewing at your food like a ventriloquist dummy laughing. Eventually you swallow it and say again, for anyone at the table who might have missed your performance, 'Oh my god, that is too hot!' Then what happens? You go straight back in and take another bite. For the love of god, stop. Give it a minute to cool down. Let's earn our place at the top of the food chain.

584
No crunching at the cinema

After more than a year of not being able to go to the movies, cinemas briefly opened again and I couldn't wait to get back into a dark room with strangers to see a film on the big screen. I steeled myself, ready to cope with the popcorn stench, but I'd forgotten about the potato chips. First comes the relentless rustling as the dirty chip-eater takes an eternity to open the bag and then comes the infernal surround-sound crunching. My god, it's so loud, shut up, people! Rip the bag open quickly and then please, for the love of god, suck your chips.

COOKING

585
Spiralisers are not magic wands

They cannot turn vegetables into pasta. Pasta is comforting. Zucchini 'noodles' and carrot 'ribbons' are good for you and they're pretty to look at but they're never going to trip your satisfaction trigger like pasta.

586
Cauliflower is not rice

It's not a pizza base either, despite what followers of the keto diet would have you believe. For the record, I like cauliflower. I find it quite tasty. Small florets tossed in olive oil, a few chilli flakes and roasted in the oven then lightly salted would be my preparation of choice if anyone's interested. I also don't mind finely grated cauliflower, it's perfectly nice. But it's not rice. How do I know? 'Cos rice isn't just nice, it's bloody delicious.

587
Don't microwave leftover pizza

I don't own a microwave because I'm concerned about radio-active 5G waves melting my synapses. Oh I'm kidding! I'm not frightened of microwaves but I do think you get a much better result reheating leftover pizza in a frying pan. Tiny bit of oil in the bottom of the frying pan, put the slices in the pan and then cover with a lid for a couple of minutes. Bottom fries up nice and crispy, while the lid creates steam and makes the cheese all soft and gooey again. Alright, I admit it, this one isn't really a rule—it's a HACK, and it's my special gift to you.

588
Go easy on the food fusion

Despite what you see on *MasterChef*, everything is not suddenly improved or made 'next level' by whacking it in a taco or a bao, or by adding a side of kimchi. Sure, kimchi is good for you and I know it's an integral part of Korean cuisine, but isn't it also just spicy wet cabbage?

589
A medjool date is not a dessert

Nor is a cup of green tea a 'great substitute' for that sweet biscuit or cake you normally have for afternoon tea. Drink as much green tea as you like, just don't try to pass it off as anything but grassy water.

590
Just say no to dukkah

It sounds delicious on paper; a mixture of nuts and seeds and spices, it looks exotic and smells exciting. Yet when you dip your bread in the oil and the dukkah, then take a bite, invariably the first thing you think is, 'Ooh, dust and gravel, num num!'

A word about the Christmas menu

Everyone thinks there are a lot of rules about what to serve up at Christmas time. Wrong.

Let's start with the turkey. Turkey is not compulsory. Some of us don't have an oven big enough to cook one, or a family big enough to eat one. And some of us think turkey is completely overrated and tasteless, no matter how much you brine it, baste it or stuff its hole with sausage mince and chestnuts. You also shouldn't feel obliged to spend hours queuing at the fish market on Christmas Eve to buy prawns. I know we're in Australia and we love waving our sunshine and fresh seafood platters in English people's faces during the festive season but the pressure to mortgage your house to pay for overpriced Christmas prawns is too much.

And can we all please calm down about the ham? I think the whole ham thing is a beat-up created by butchers. They put signs

71

everywhere saying Don't forget to order your Christmas ham *and everyone falls for it, thinking,* Yes, that's right, we need an entire ham. *Ordinarily a dozen slices from the deli would suffice, but at Christmas time, suddenly we become Henry the Eighth and require an entire haunch of pig for our banqueting table.*

So the only rule is to cook whatever you and your family like to eat. Obviously make sure potatoes are included in some form, be it roasted, mashed, chipped or saladed. No need to be the potato grinch and ruin Christmas for everyone.

———————————————————→

RECIPE WEBSITES

591
Cakes require more than two ingredients

If you don't have time to bake a cake that's absolutely fine, but don't kid yourself that you can cheat the system by using a two-ingredient recipe 'hack'! The internet would have you believe you can make a delicious cake from a tin of pineapple and a cup of flour. But that's fake news. You don't get a cake, you get a rubbery lump of pineapple-flavoured wallpaper paste. You'd be better off just eating the tin of pineapple.

592
Enough with things in mugs and cobs

I want to eat my cake from a plate not a mug. I'm not an animal. And I see no reason to cook anything in one of those round white loaves of bread, otherwise known as 'a cob'. I've no objection to the cob loaf or to serving a cob loaf *with* your meal, but what is this obsession websites have with inserting the meal into the cob itself? I don't want my lasagne in a cob or beef stroganoff in a cob and I definitely don't want chicken korma in a cob. The only thing that should be served in a cob is French onion dip at a seventies party.

593
No more cheesecake recipes

Every possible iteration of a cheesecake already exists. There is nothing new you can do with it; everything's been covered. The base can be made from biscuit or breakfast cereal or gluten-free kitty litter, or it can be baseless; the filling can be cream cheese or ricotta or yoghurt or sour cream or all of the above with absolutely anything folded through it from Mars Bars to miso soup. Everything's been done, and the bottom line is, you can't go past a good baked cheesecake anyway. So everyone focus on mastering that and please stop taking up space on the web with 'new' cheesecake suggestions, there's almost no room for porn anymore.

594
Don't believe the hype about red velvet cake

Red velvet cake tricks me every time. It looks and sounds other-worldly, like a cake made in heaven. And yet it tastes like ... nobody's really sure? The best I can describe it is, a half-strength chocolate cake, with red in it?

THE GREAT OUTDOORS

595
Stick to sandwiches at a picnic

Once a simple, pleasant, outdoor lunch on a rug, the picnic has somehow morphed into a complicated ordeal of platters and salads and expensive, oily comestibles from delis that leak all over everything else in your bag. A picnic is far more enjoyable when you're not forced to wrestle with cutlery or balance a plate on your lap or worry about that ticking salmonella time bomb that comes in the form of a greasy barbeque chicken. Keep it manageable and stick to hand-held, dripless food like old-school sandwiches (cut into triangles) and a thermos of sweet tea. It's important to leave people with one hand free to grab at the hat that's threatening to fly off their head or to remove the hair that keeps blowing into their mouth. Maybe have some biscuits or cupcakes or even fruit (apologies to my sister) for afters, but no elaborate cakes or anything that needs 'plating up'.

* *Obviously this is a rule for white people. I don't pretend to speak for other cultures. If you've got a nonna or a yaya etc. you can disregard this rule and enjoy your arancini or your dolmades, or even your whole roasted lamb on a spit. Those old dames are like one-woman catering trucks; the ease with which they can distribute food to the masses is extraordinary. They make Jesus and his 'fish sandwiches for 5000' look like an amateur.*

THE ART OF ENTERTAINMENT

PODCASTS

Everyone's got a podcast these days; I am no exception. I make one and I enjoy many. Unlike film or television or theatre, the podcast is lean, easy to produce and quick to turn around, which makes it the ideal piece of content for a pandemic. Podcasters are like the preppers of showbiz, sitting in their well-equipped bunkers, ready to go at a moment's notice. So praise be to the podcast, it's a great thing. Now let's keep it great with a few simple rules.

596
Have an idea

Many people can witter on about nothing but only some people can make those witterings interesting. Unfortunately, the few who *can* seem to have inspired the many who can't. I'm not saying you shouldn't do a podcast—by all means, get a microphone and get involved—just make sure you have a plan, something a little more detailed than 'I'm going to press record and start riffing.' Riffing is fine, provided you have an objective and an exit strategy.

597
One hour is ample

Any more than that and it's not really entertainment; it's you enjoying the sound of your own voice and/or exposing your own loneliness and desperate need to talk at people.

598
Just start

No need for long preambles or meandering apologies about why a new 'ep didn't drop' last week. Your listener gets it, and my guess is they also have many other podcasts in their library, so if you have to skip a week, I reckon they'll be okay; they have plenty of other content to fill the giant void your missing podcast has left.

599
Know who the murderer is before
releasing your cold case podcast

Most fans of true crime podcasts would be familiar with that uneasy feeling you get around week four or five when you start to suspect that a podcast is going nowhere. It's no longer moving forward but rather seems to be following a lot of tangents with no real substance. That's about the same time you google the case and realise you've been suckered and the crime remains unsolved. Keeping the tension alive by withholding information is all well and good—provided you actually *have* that information up your sleeve and plan to do a big Scooby Doo-style reveal in the final episode: 'And guess what, listener, turns out it was the caretaker, Mr Wickles, all along!' You're making a podcast, not a French film; please have an ending.

600
Not everyone can be Dax Shepard/Wil Anderson

If you are a well-loved celebrity or comedian, you might want to think carefully before starting your own podcast where you interview other celebrities and comedians. The celebrity-host-interviewing-celebrity-guest genre really started to eat itself during the pandemic. Maybe you're better off staying as that celeb who pops up occasionally as a really entertaining guest on other people's podcasts. Believe it or not, a lot of celebs are actually much better guests than they are hosts. Good hosts are happy to let their guests do some of the talking.

601
Podcasts should be off limits as sources of content for 'news' websites

One of the best things about podcasts when they first hit the scene was the fact that guests were so much more relaxed and prepared to speak freely. People said all sorts of things they'd never say during a regular press interview. It felt like the podcast was the black market of inside information. But then the tabloids started trawling the podcasts for content and now guests are starting to be a little more wary about what they say. Stop ruining it for everyone, clickbait-makers.

602
You get what you get

The vast majority of podcasts are free, so while it's all very well for me to lay down rules saying you should do this and you shouldn't do that, most podcasters aren't getting paid, not in Australia anyway. Which means they can do what they like, and we should be grateful for the free content. As my good friend and prolific podcaster Dave O'Neil often likes to remind listeners, 'You get what you get, and you don't get upset.'

603
Don't treat your friend like a podcast

This is a rule for people who like to call you for chats from their car. Obviously they're bored, maybe they've forgotten to cue up the next episode of their favourite podcast, so why not kill some time phoning a friend? And that's totally fine. My objection is to the way they cut you off the minute they reach their destination. Car-callers should have the decency to park and remain in the stationary vehicle long enough to allow the conversation to reach its natural and polite conclusion.

REALITY TELEVISION

Curiously, the pandemic did not kill off reality television. In fact, much like the radioactive spider that bit Peter Parker, the virus only seems to have made it stronger. Accordingly, I am now obliged to include these rules as part of the actual book, as opposed to relegating them to a special removable section like I did in 488 Rules for Life.

604
No need to recap what happened three minutes ago

Most reality shows now contain as many minutes of recapping as they do of actual content. By all means, recap what happened on the previous episode—no one minds a bit of 'previously on . . . ' work—but it's insulting to assume your viewer can't remember what happened before the commercial break. Stop dragging it out, producers, or more of us are going to switch off and just start reading James Weir's highly entertaining online recaps of your dumb shows instead.

605
Don't top up your fillers right before filming

Remember the camera already adds ten pounds, so if you go pumping additional fat into your face then you are going to look insane. Respect the viewers and stop hurting our eyes. And while you're respecting stuff, maybe respect your own face and how young it is. There's simply no need for fillers when your face is still full of collagen and rubbery youthfulness. I should be looking at you and fighting the urge to press my finger into your cheek so I can watch it spring back like a perfectly cooked sponge. Instead, I'm fighting the urge to google Lady Penelope from *Thunderbirds* to compare whose face looks harder and more plasticky.

606
Stop blaming the edit

I realise they can do a lot in the edit, but they can't make you look like you're shouting and saying stupid things if you didn't shout and say stupid things. That's on you.

607
No kissing until the final episode

The Bachelor should not be able to sample the goods until he commits and makes his choice at the end of the series. As it stands now, the show is less of a 'search for love' and more of an inside look at life with a harem. Week after week we are forced to watch the Bach indiscriminately crack on to every woman in the house. It's like a PG-rated orgy, where everyone lines up in an orderly fashion and waits to tap in. And it's completely gross. It also supports my hypothesis that Covid-19 started not in a wet market but on the set of *The Bachelor Wuhan*. I'm not being a prude and a wowser (well, I am but with good reason), I'm advocating for better television. Imagine if they weren't allowed to slaver all over one another like Kath Day and Kel Knight? There would actually be some unresolved sexual tension in the house (sorry, 'mansion') and therefore, as viewers, we would be so much more invested in the outcome. Who knows, the contestants might even prove to be interesting if they were forced to keep talking to each other and couldn't resort to straddling one another and dry humping the minute they run out of conversation.

Ross and Rachel didn't get it on until season two, episode seven of *Friends*, thus proving my point that viewers are quite happy to wait.

* *Obviously I'm not just talking about The Bachelor, I'm also referring to The Bachelorette, and the idiots on MAFS, and the ones on the island and in paradise; this no-kissing rule applies to all the shows. Except Lego Masters—Brickman and Hamish should definitely kiss every episode.*

A word about the arts industry

It's all too easy to make jokes about 'the arts' not being a real job; I do it all the time. But let's not forget that all the content we've been so voraciously consuming during lockdowns is largely brought to you by the arts and entertainment industry. I'm not, for a minute, comparing artists to frontline healthcare workers, or suggesting we stand outside at 7 pm every night and bang pots and pans to salute musicians and actors and filmmakers for getting us through the pandemic. I'm saying, just spare a thought for the industry next time you skip the credits on Netflix. (No judgement by the way, who doesn't skip?)

At the time of writing, live performance was still largely dormant, to the point where my own tour seems to have been renamed 'Kitty Flanagan—Rescheduled'. And I'm sure I'm not the only performer who'd like to thank anyone who bought a ticket to a show and is still holding on to it. Your solidarity is much appreciated and I assure you the shows will go on. Eventually. Fingers crossed. No, they will. I'm sure of it. I'm a hundred per cent certain they will probably happen—in which case we might need a couple of rules.

FRIENDS OF THE SHOW

608
Don't be afraid to lie

Any decent performer knows when things haven't gone great. And what we need after a dud show is a bit of bolstering from our friends; a white lie and a white wine will do nicely. What we don't need are any of those 'clever' avoidance comments. Hoary old chestnuts like: 'Oh my goodness! What about you?' Or worse, 'Oh wow . . . so how do *you* think it went?' We're not idiots, we know these things are code for, 'I have nothing good to say about what you just did up there.'

609
A free ticket comes with one condition

When you accept a free ticket to a show, you are obliged to send a text the minute the show is over. Whether it's music, comedy, theatre, whatever—as the lights come up, take out your phone and tap this:

> *Thank you SO much for the tickets,*
> *we really enjoyed ourselves.*

Maybe you hated the show, maybe the band was a train wreck, maybe the comedian paced around so much you got motion sickness—it doesn't matter. You took the freebie and, sadly, nothing in life is truly free. So pay the piper. Send that disingenuous text pronto. If it pains you to tell such lies, then next time don't take the freebie. And if you were foolish enough to accept a free ticket to some performance art, I can't help you; clearly you're a masochist.

ZOOM GIGS

610
Zoom shows aren't fun for anyone

Hats off to the bosses who tried to do something nice for their staff during Covid, like organising a Zoom Christmas party or a Friday afternoon fun session with a comedian as the entertainment. Speaking as the comedian/entertainment at several such events, firstly I would like to thank you for giving me some much-needed work. Secondly, I'd like to offer my condolences to anyone who had to sit through one of these appalling 'shows'. I think it's the closest I've come to feeling like the mad lady who shouts at anyone and no one in particular on a tram or a street corner. In my defence, I will say that it is very difficult to perform stand-up comedy sitting alone at your desk, all the while watching the 'number of attendees' tick down in the bottom of the screen as, one by one, people lose interest and French exit the Zoom party.

SPECIAL PANDEMIC TIMES SECTION
ZOOM ETIQUETTE

Even though I no longer work in an office, I still find myself having to participate in a lot of Zoom meetings. But I know I'm getting off lightly compared to those who are forced to use Zoom on a daily basis—to you people I say, sorry for your loss, you will never get that time back. I spend most of my time in Zoom meetings scribbling notes about how we could be doing it better. That's why there are a lot of rules in this section, starting with the most obvious of them all:

611
Every interaction doesn't have to be a Zoom meeting

Use all the time you save by not commuting to think carefully about whether you really need to have a Zoom meeting. Perhaps an email or a phone call will suffice. Phone calls are an extremely efficient form of communication and, best of all, on the phone it's easier to hide how bored or annoyed you are. Whereas on Zoom you have to constantly smile and nod and look genuinely interested. It's exhausting.

612
No Zooms before 9.30 am

Anything earlier than that is impossible; I'm still stuck commuting from the kitchen to the laundry.

613
Go easy on the jargon

No one wants to 'jump on a Zoom'. People who say 'jump on a Zoom' tend to be the same people who say 'circle back' and 'can you speak *to* that?' instead of 'can you talk about that?' If you use that sort of lingo, please allow everyone extra time to momentarily turn our cameras off so we can all roll our eyes and give the screen the finger.

614
Don't record a Zoom meeting

When was the last time you heard someone say, 'Hey, remember that classic Zoom we had in May 2021 about OH&S? I recall we said some pretty great stuff, I wouldn't mind looking back at it.' That's right, never.

615
If you call the meeting, run the meeting

In other words, have an agenda and get cracking. It's tedious when everyone is present but no one takes charge. Awkwardness prevails as people wave hello to one another and feel obliged to fill the dead air with arbitrary comments like, 'Oh hey, Janice . . . wow, look at you . . . you've got a hat on, is it cold where you are?' Take control and call this wretched thing to order. The sooner you start, the sooner we can all 'jump off' this Zoom.

616
No wannabe pilots at the Zoom meeting

It's really distracting when people don a full aviator-style headset complete with mic attachment for a simple Zoom meeting. I'm sure the sound quality is improved but I just can't take you seriously, Captain. Be sure to let us all know when you've finished your pre-flight checks and you're ready for take-off.

617
Don't angle your screen so everyone
is looking at your ceiling

Or your nostrils. Or the underside of your chin. We're all screen-savvy enough now to know that your camera needs to be at eye level or slightly above. No one expects you to have a full studio set up —just face the light and put your laptop on a pile of books. Think of it as a great way to finally use that stack of recipe books you've never opened.

618
Keep one small corner of your house tidy

Normally during Zoom meetings, I spend a lot of time squinting into the screen trying to work out exactly what's in that pile of crap behind you. Is that clean or dirty laundry in the basket? Is that a dog ferreting around in that scramble of computer leads or ... a weird-looking baby? I'm not suggesting that you clean up your house, god no, but one of the few good things about Zoom is that you can present as perfectly tidy with little to no effort. Simply push all of your mess to one side and angle the camera away from it.

619
Don't over-style your Zoom background

Tidy is one thing, but strategically placed awards and objets d'art are another. No need to drag potted palms and bowls of feature lemons into Zoom Corner; you want it neat and tidy but not styled for a reveal on *The Block*. Anytime someone comments on your background, you've gone too far. I know, I know, it's a very fine line, and if it makes you feel better, I still don't have it right myself. That's why I really wish we could forget Zoom altogether and bring back the landline. Oh, the landline, such clarity, not to mention that thrilling element of risk during a thunderstorm!

This rule is slightly different if you've been tapped to do a Zoom cross on television. In that case, you want to take some time to stage a visually pleasing and, where possible, relevant set. For example, if you're a doctor, have some doctor paraphernalia in shot; perhaps your degree framed on the wall, or a few medical texts or journals on the desk—just a little something that sets the scene. It's hard enough watching a person speak via Zoom on television; it's even worse when they're sat in front of a bare white wall or a closed venetian blind. This makes it feel less like you're watching an expert and more like you're watching a hostage video.

620
Make jokes at your own risk

The sound quality is terrible on Zoom, so be prepared for your hilarious rejoinder to be met with blank faces followed by 'What?' You'll be forced to repeat what you said, and with every repetition your joke will get less and less funny and you'll wish you'd never said anything in the first place.

621
One hour, no extensions

If you can't get it done in an hour, quit the meeting and have a long hard think about how you could have been more efficient. People have bladders. And short attention spans. Not to mention Netflix and a dozen other streaming services to work their way through.

622
Take a break whenever you need one

Feel free to wander off during a Zoom meeting—after all, 95 per cent of meetings aren't essential anyway, so you won't miss a thing. Just be sure to mute yourself and turn the camera off before leaving the room. That way it looks like it might be a technical issue rather than what it really is—you bored out of your scone and going to the fridge for the fiftieth time to see if anything good has magically appeared in there. When you return and put your camera back on, remember to look concerned and say, 'Sorry guys, don't know what happened there, I lost you for a minute. Am I back? Have you got me?'

623
Make friends with the mute button

Muting allows you to be present in the meeting while still doing other stuff, such as watching something on YouTube or texting your friends. Muting is also mandatory when you leave to take a toilet break. Mandatory.

624
Social Zooms need structure too

Zoom has certainly proved to be an excellent, albeit awkward, way to get friends and family together during these times of forced separation. The social Zoom, however, can quickly run out of steam if you don't have a plan. Once that initial flurry of excited waving at the screen dies down and people have stopped shouting and showing what drink they're having, no one is ever quite sure what to do next. Should you ask a question to the group and watch chaos ensue as everyone tries to answer at once? Or do you direct your enquiry to a specific individual and risk it becoming a private conversation with half a dozen silent observers? Give your gathering some kind of direction by conducting a trivia contest or playing a parlour game. In the case of a birthday, a custom quiz about the birthday person is always a hit. Use the time you would normally take to get ready for a night out to find some trivia questions online, google some parlour games or rip a quiz out of the newspaper. Everyone will adore you for it.

SOCIALISING

CATCHING UP

625
Don't be passive about making a plan

When you arrange to meet up with someone, deciding on where to go can often drag on longer than the eventual catch-up itself. You might think it makes you sound easygoing to chime in with 'Whatever suits you, works for me!' But opting out like that actually makes you really annoying. Admit it, you're being lazy and hoping someone else will do all the heavy lifting and arrange everything. I know that's true because I do it all the time. I don't like the pressure of having to suggest a place to meet up, but guess what? Neither does anyone else. I've realised that it's a bold and admirable act to be the person who suggests where everyone should meet up. It's also smart. Get in first and you can choose locations that are on your side of town or, even better, within walking distance of your own house. Be the first responder of the catch-up plan.

626
First to arrive gets the banquette

Whoever arrives first gets to sit on the comfortable spongy seat against the wall. That's your reward for punctuality. Latecomers must be punished and forced to take whatever on-trend chair substitute is on offer, be it a cold metal stool, a rustic timber stump or an ironically 'trashy' milk crate with or without a cushion. If you arrive at the same time, then you're looking at a *Hunger Games* meets musical-chairs-when-the-music-stops situation. Run, push and shove your way through in order to claim the banquette.

627
Be specific about the catch-up

Take a tip from my good friend and socialising wizard, Julia Zemiro. She occasionally likes to arrange a drinks-meet by keeping it specific: 'Let's meet up for a drink. One sensible drink.' There are so many things to like about this invitation. Firstly, she makes clear she's not suggesting a big night out where we're all going to get wasted and lose our shoes. Secondly, it indicates you should feel comfortable about driving your own vehicle to the meet, no need to uber or worry about how you're getting home. Thirdly, it puts a cap on the night and makes the idea of a midweek catch-up far more appealing. And finally, it leaves you free to honour any other plans or obligations you may have made for later on in the evening. Even if those plans were just to head home and watch your programs and eat that delicious soup you've been thinking about all day.

*   *Clearly this tip is not for anyone under thirty, for whom the thought of capping the night in any way is anathema.*

628
Cancel plans with alacrity

Never be afraid to call and cancel. If you feel like cancelling, there's every chance the other person secretly wants to cancel too. Many people love a surprise cancellation. It might even be one of the greatest gifts you can give. The non-canceller now has a night to themselves *and* the moral high ground, so they can revel in that smug feeling of being the good friend who was 'totally planning to show up'.

FURRY FRIENDS

629
No birthday hats on dogs

In fact, no outfits on pets. Nothing channels a pet's inner sadness like being forced to stagger around 'dressed' as a piece of pizza or a princess. I will make an exception for the costume that turns a sausage dog into a teddy bear running at you—that should be included with every purchase of a dachshund.

630
Pick one up for the team

If you're a dog owner, do the world a favour and occasionally pick up a 'coldie' at the park. To be clear, I'm talking about an old dog poo, not a beer, and not all the time—just every now and then. It's a noble and selfless act to pick up a poo your dog didn't do. You're saving someone else from stepping in it, you're making sure the dog park stays a dog park and you're keeping your own balance sheet tidy. Because no matter how vigilant you are, there has probably been at least one occasion where your dog has plopped somewhere without you realising it. So remember this terrific saying of mine: 'See a dog poo, pick it up, all day long you'll have good luck!'

631
Always state your whereabouts when talking to someone on the phone

This rule is specifically for dog owners when they're out walking their dogs, and it's included at my sister's request. Apparently, she and I were talking on the phone one day but I neglected to mention that I was walking my dogs at the time. So when I shouted, 'Gotta go, there's a poo happening!' and hung up, she had no idea the poo in question belonged to one of my dogs. Rather, she assumed I'd become some sort of chronic oversharer who liked to keep everyone apprised of my movements.

MEETING AND GREETING

632
No more elbow bumping

In Australia we've never had a standardised greeting. Some people kiss, some people double kiss; there are huggers and handshakers and combinations of all of the above. It's a minefield. And now, thanks to the coronavirus, we also have this ill-conceived elbow-bump gesture thrown into the mix. Part chicken dance, part Thai boxing attack, the elbow whack refuses to catch on. For good reason. It looks ridiculous and it's anything but perfunctory. An elbow bump is always followed by a thirty-second postmortem where everyone involved feels obliged to acknowledge how weird and random it is that we have to knock elbows now. No one is capable of just bumping and moving on. You see it whenever politicians gather: they jostle and stump rub each other and narrate the proceedings, 'Heh, heh, alright, no we can't shake anymore can we, here we go, elbow bumping, that's the way, heh heh, ahhhh, that's a bit of fun, isn't it? Good stuff.' Just stop it. We gave it a crack, it didn't work. Let it go.

633
Touch nothing, touch no one

It feels like a good way to greet each other in times of disease would be to channel *Star Trek*'s Mr Spock and do a version of the Vulcan salute. But maybe close your fingers. So you end up raising a flat hand with your palm facing out. It's easy, it's socially distant, and having your hand up like a stop sign conveys a very clear message: 'Halt, come no further, don't share your germs with me.' Although, you'll need to be careful with this one; don't flick it up too casually or it could become less Mr Spock and more Mr Hitler.

634
Announce your proposed style of greeting

When the pandemic subsides and we invariably make a return to the superspreading hugging and kissing combinations of old, I suggest we start heralding our greeting of choice. Let your acquaintance know with a clear announcement what to expect and where to expect it: 'Coming in on the left, single kiss' or 'I'm a hugger, get ready!' This avoids any misunderstanding, and uncomfortable moments like the time I misjudged my uncle's approach and ended up kissing him on the lips.

If you're on social media, you might want to think about adding it to your profile: *Hi, my name is Rodney, I'm a non-hugger and my preferred greeting is a tip of the hat.*

635
Avoid the awkward double goodbye

After a night out, when everyone is standing outside the restaurant or theatre or wherever, about to part ways, before any farewelling begins someone must first ask the question, 'Which way are you headed?' Only then, once people have indicated the direction they're going, should you say your goodbyes. This stops you having your big hugs and emotional scenes outside the restaurant, then realising you're all walking off in the same direction, with everyone thinking, *Damn, do we walk in silence now or do we have to start up a new conversation?* And then having to do a second round of goodbyes.

636
Never introduce yourself by saying, 'You don't remember me, do you?'

It's aggressive and unfair, especially if you haven't seen the person since you went to school with them thirty years ago. No one looks the same as they did at school. And we haven't all been stalking one another on Facebook, so a lot of us are unaware of how people have changed. The correct and polite way to introduce yourself to someone you haven't seen for a long time is to state your name and immediately identify how you know one another. For example, 'Hello, I'm Olivia Jackson, we went to school together.' Or, 'Hello, I'm Sandy, we met at Betty and Kenickie's wedding.' It's a much friendlier way to kick off a chat. A conversation isn't something you need to 'win', there is nothing to be gained by opening with a gotcha moment like, 'Hah, I knew you wouldn't remember me!'

SPECIAL FOLLOW-UP RULE FOR THE MARRIED LADIES

637
Use your maiden name

If you haven't seen someone since school, please use your maiden name when you introduce yourself. Using your married name is perverse and unnecessarily cryptic. If you genuinely want to catch up and converse, then let's dispense with the tedious *Sale of the Century* 'Who Am I?' game up front and get to the chats.

SEXY TAIMES

638
Women like men with a sense of humour, and a neck

Unless you're planning to pull a plough, you probably don't need to overdevelop your trapezius muscles. So take a day off from the traps, guys, don't let your neck disappear. And while you're at it, don't go stupid on 'arm day' or 'leg day' either. It's a fine line between being a Hemsworth and looking like you have an entire family of Very Hungry Caterpillars sticking out all over your torso.

639
Sex doesn't have to be spicy

The compulsion to spice things up in the bedroom is a purely human condition.

No other species feels the need to get kooky and experimental with sex. You don't see lions out on the savannah whipping one another with branches across the hindquarters. The giraffes aren't tapping the elephant on the next plain to have a three-some and I've certainly never seen hippos rolling around in the mud sucking each other's feet—and if there was ever a creature designed to fit a foot in its mouth, it's a hippo. Bears might cover themselves in honey but I'm pretty sure it's a food thing not a sex thing. And even if it was some kind of sticky bear foreplay, they don't have bed sheets and mattresses to worry about. There's no shame in being good at plain sex.

640
No one likes Marathon Man in the bedroom

I'm not suggesting you should be racing to finish a hundred-metre sprint. But a solid 1500-metre performance is certainly preferable to a 42-kilometre endurance event—especially given that you're not offering any drinks breaks, time-outs or half-time entertainment. And this supposedly sexy promise some people like to make of 'I am going to keep you up all night!' That's less of a turn-on and more like a threat they make at Guantanamo.

641
Never tell a woman to calm down

Unless, of course, you're trying to get her to kick right off. I'd suggest using a coded alternative like, 'Perhaps we could have a cup of tea and talk about this some more.'

SPECIAL PANDEMIC TIMES SECTION
SOME SPECIFICS

PANDEMIC RULES FOR BIG BUSINESS

642
Stop telling us we are all in this together

This is a rule for banks, television networks and other large corporations (but mostly banks). Now, more than ever in these 'unprecedented times', you can take your wafty, soft-focus, hand-holdy ads and piss right off. Anyone who's ever tried to apply for any kind of loan or credit or extension from a bank would know there is no hand-holding, there is no understanding, there's certainly no friendly, personal bank manager trained to listen to and assess your individual circumstances. There's only the cent-ralised call centre and the algorithm. They're in this together. And I'm pretty sure they're doing okay.

643
Don't pretend to be my friend

At the beginning of the pandemic, I got a flurry of emails from companies and stores who were all very keen to be my friend and help get me through these tough times. The CEO of Woolworths started emailing me personally and including a picture of himself. 'Dear Kitty,' he wrote, before going on to tell me all sorts of tales about the crazy capers the Woolies staff had been up to that week, or maybe it was that capers were selling at a crazy price, I can't quite remember (he did go on a bit, I think he might have been lonely). Furniture store West Elm also emailed to say they had my back. Thanks, guys! Specifically, they wrote: 'Whether it's keeping the kids entertained or getting creative in the kitchen, West Elm is here to help.' I was delighted. I wrote back to let them know I didn't have any kids but that I could sure use a new sofa given that I was doing a lot more sitting on my arse these days. Maybe my email went to their junk folder, I don't know, but I never did hear back from them.

I guess the clue that these were all friendship scams was there the whole time, in the subject headers that said, 'Do not reply to this email'.

PANDEMIC RULES FOR CELEBRITIES

644
Be careful who you tell to 'relax and enjoy the lockdown'

Many people are not in a privileged enough position to take an indefinite salary holiday. So tread carefully when you talk about how much you're enjoying time with the family and the 'benefits' of being forced to take a bit of downtime.

645
If you get an email from Gal Gadot, move it swiftly to junk

Turns out celebrities singing 'Imagine' acapella while earnestly gazing into their iPhones was not what people needed to help them cope with lockdown. I'm sure Gal's heart was in the right place but, seriously, imagine all the peee-pull (celebrities) who now wish they'd thought twice about agreeing to be part of that mawkish display of desperation and neediness.

AND FINALLY . . .

SOME STRONG SUGGESTIONS

To finish up, I would like to offer some suggestions. These are things that I thought were too obtuse (even for me) to include as rules. But then I thought, maybe I could just strongly suggest them and see what happens.

Throw your mattress out sooner

This suggestion really only applies to a tiny percentage of the population. I'm talking about the people who discard their mattresses by tossing them in back alleys. Setting aside the illegal dumping issue, what is going on with those mattresses? Have you really been sleeping on that thing up until now? I have never seen a discarded 'street' mattress that doesn't look like a crime scene. Every one of them looks like it should have been thrown out at least three murders ago.

No Uber Eats before noon

If I'm completely honest, I wanted to make this suggestion simply 'No Uber Eats', but I dialled it down lest people throw my book against a wall and dump it in a germy street library. I realise my objection to Uber Eats is completely irrational: 'Tonight, I'll be having food that arrives cold and looks like it has fallen off the back of a bike and been kicked the last hundred metres down the road to my house.' Not that I would ever blame the drivers for doing that. It must be such a dispiriting job. Riding around risking your life on a bicycle or moped at night, fetching other people's food, and being paid tuppence to do it.

I strongly suggest patronising local restaurants who have their own delivery drivers or maybe even going to pick up the food yourself (and obviously by 'pick it up yourself', I mean, send your partner or bribe your flatmate to pick it up for you). You'll get your food faster and hotter, and the restaurant will get a bigger cut of the profits. But if you won't do that, could we at least agree that you won't use Uber Eats to bring you breakfast. I mean, come on, how hard is toast?

Don't waste money on specialty boxed chocolates

The routine for eating fancy boxed chocolates goes like this: make your selection, take a small bite, pull a face, then dump it back in its moulded plastic hole and move on to the next one. Eventually you find yourself staring at a tray of half-eaten truffles, fondants and pralines, which you stash somewhere and forget about until the day comes when you're desperate and have no other treats in the house. So you pull them out and do another round of nibbling, face-pulling and discarding.

If you're thinking about giving chocolates as a gift, I strongly suggest wrapping up a classic bar, something like a full-size Snickers or a Cherry Ripe, or even a simple block of Caramello, and if it's someone really special, why not gift them all three? I know if I received a gift like that I'd be rather surprised—but I'd also be delighted.

AND ONE STUPID SUGGESTION

I am well aware that this one is ridiculous, I just thought it might be fun to end the book by hitting a wasps' nest with a stick and running away . . .

Mandatory vasectomies at fifty

Gents, feel free to put the book down, I reckon it's safe to assume you won't like this one. My thinking is that mandatory vasectomies in middle age would be the great equaliser. It might force men to think differently about their relationships if they, too, had a ticking biological clock. Women can't keep having kids up until the day they die so it seems unfair that men should be allowed to keep spraying it around into their seventies and eighties. It's really not fair on the kids either. Imagine being at school when a kid looks out the classroom window and shouts, 'Look! There's an old man in pyjamas weeing on the monkey bars . . . oh I'm sorry, I mean—hey Byron, your dad's here!'

Acknowledgements

It's only a skinny little book but there are always a lot of people to thank.

Firstly, the team at Allen & Unwin: Kelly, Angela, Jo, Dannielle, Garry and especially Simon for accommodating all my last-minute changes! Thank you.

Penny and Sophie—double FBs to you both, it's such a delight working with people who make you laugh hard, there's nothing quite like it.

Tohby, we got there. Once again, you took a plain little book and made it special.

To my readers, Glenn and Bex, thank you for the feedback and especially for the reassurance.

Artie Laing, what can I say? You're the best in the biz.

And a very special thankyou to Monica Johansson, who allowed me to include her banana rule, Liz Winters for her thoughts on TikTok and Sam Pang for teaching me Rule 635.

Most of all, I'd like to say a massive thankyou to everyone who bought the original book, *488 Rules for Life*, and made it such a hit. You are the only reason I was allowed to have another crack at this. Socially distant, air high fives to you all. xx

Index

to *488 Rules for Life* and *More Rules for Life*

Numbers in entries refer to **rule numbers**

abbreviations, in texts 557
active wear 34–5
advice and inspiration 26–30
affection, public demonstrations of
    183–4
ageing 44–53, 125, 248–52
   see also Baby Boomers; Generation
     X; Generation Z; Millennials
ailments, telling others about 48
air travel *see* flying
Airbnbs 500–4
airfryers 545
amenities, in Airbnbs 501, 503
Americanisms, in conversation 571
anecdotes 515, 524
appliances 505, 545
armchairs, in the bedroom 498
the arts *see* entertainment
'ass' versus 'arse' 572
Australia Day 407
avocados 128, 163, 544

Baby Boomers 510, 515–24
babysitting 209
bad breath 574
bakeries 539
bananas 171, 580
bands, reforming of 508
banks 642
banquettes 626
baristas 550
basins, in the bathroom 11
the bathroom 10–20
  see also the toilet
beaches, minimum distance between
    towels on 417

bedrooms 498–9, 530
beverages, in the toilet 17
big business, in the pandemic 642–3
bins, in the bathroom 18
birth videos 208
birthdays 69–70, 368–70, 560
black leggings 33
black tapware 440
blogging 335–9
bodybuilding 638
books 429–33
boxing 38
bridesmaids 383, 389
bucatini 142
buddhas, in the garden 497
buffets 147, 148
bunching, when flying 110, 112
buses *see* public transport

cacao 131
cafes and restaurants 156–69,
    549–55
  changing babies in 213
  claiming the banquette 626
  mothers in 211
  see also dining out
cake recipes 591
cancellations 364, 628
carob 132
cars *see* driving
cash registers, in stores 547
catching up 625–8
cats 236, 239–40
cauliflower 'rice' 586
celebrations *see* parties and
    celebrations

celebrities 418, 600, 644–5
change rooms (in clothes shops)
     305–9
change rooms (in gyms) 40–2
cheese knives 543
cheesecake recipes 593
children 101, 104, 229, 290
  see also parenting
children's parties 230–3, 561
chipmunking 144
Christmas 65, 404
cinema *see* the movies
cleaners 6, 7
cleaning up, in the kitchen 24
cleavage 241
clichés 26, 28, 58, 437
'clown', as a verb 75
co-workers, greeting of 63
cobs 592
cocoa 131
coffee, drinking vessels for 160
communication 556–61
  see also conversation; email;
       language; texting
consumers 543–5
contouring 268
conversation 90–9
  checking your phone while talking to
       someone 317
  curbing the use of Americanisms
       571
  derailing sport conversations 358
  in the same room 516
  introducing yourself 636, 637
  keeping food regimes to yourself
       137
  on first dates 180
  on public transport 126
  talking with your mouth full 144
  things to avoid asking a teenager
       569
  things to avoid saying about yourself
       567
  things to avoid to try to sound
       interesting 568

  with children on the phone 215
  with shop assistants 294
  see also language; meeting and
       greeting
convertible cars 119
cooking 525, 585–94
cooking shows 444–6
coughing, on planes 108
couples 183–94, 195
courtesy waves 114–15
Covid-19 *see* the pandemic
crime podcasts 599
culture *see* books; museums and art
       galleries; reality television;
       theatre; zoos
cycling 36, 367

dancing, in the office 65
dark chocolate 130
dating *see* relationships and dating
death 558
denim 253–4
desk, eating at your 66
dessert bars 446
'din-dins' 84
dining out 149–55, 552–4
  see also cafes and restaurants
dinner parties 371–80
dishwashers 21–3
dogs 234–8, 629–31
doors, on bathrooms 10, 15
dress code, for weddings 387
driving 114–21
drug language 80
dukkah 590

e-cards 559
eating 138–48, 580–4
  endangered species 535
  in the bedroom 530
  things in mugs and cobs 592
  see also cooking; dining out; food
egg poachers 545
elbow bumping 632

email 323–5
  e-cards 559
  from celebrities during lockdown
    645
  late responses to 556
  shared email addresses for couples
    194
  using clichés in 58
  using 'e-meeting' 59
  using the reply-all button 57
emojis, in texts 187
endangered species 535
entertainment
  books 429–33
  friends of performers 608–9
  museums and art galleries 419–24
  podcasts 596–603
  reality television 434–46, 604–7
  theatre 428
  zoom gigs 610
  zoos 425–7
escalators, showing affection on 183
exemption letters, for masks 579
exercise gear 33–7
  see also working out
expectations, lowering of 447
eyebrows 271

face fillers 605
Facebook see social media
false eyelashes 269
family histories 518–19
family photos 5
farting 190, 513
fashion 241–73
  dress code for weddings 387
  in the eighties 528
  keeping holiday attire for holidays
    409
  masks as fashion statements 576
  see also makeup; piercings;
    sunglasses; tattoos
fathers 209
'feed', as a noun 76
feet, in old age 46

fireworks, on New Year's Eve 405–6
first dates 175–82
First World problems 74
flags, as curtains 8
flirting, with waitstaff 49
flying 100–13
food 128–38, 580–95
  chasing children with 225
  food fights in movies 289
  in the office 66–70
  in the toilet 17, 18
  jam in plastic packets 161
  nuts and rice crackers on first dates
    182
  spaghetti 141
  see also cooking; dining out; eating;
    fruit; popcorn
food dehydrators 545
football jerseys 2, 242
footballers 361–3, 492
free tickets 609
friends
  calling friends from a car 603
  catching up with 625–8
  of couples 195
  of performers 608–9
  zoom meetings with 624
fruit 170–4, 228
furniture, in Airbnbs 504
fusion food 588

gardens 496–7
gender-reveal parties 222
Generation X 507–14
Generation Z 529–34
glamour photos 9
glasses 50, 511
golf 491
goodbyes 366, 635
greens, in restaurants 554
greetings 632–7
grieving 558
guacamole 129
guavas 135

haggling, for a bargain 411
hair 44, 53, 267
hair dye, for old men 53
Halloween 400–3
Hammer Pants 247
hand sanitiser 540
'happy place', referring to your 85
headphones 104, 123
headsets, in zoom meetings 616
hiving, at dinner parties 378, 379
hoarding 536
hobbies, monetising 548
holidays and travel 408–18, 500–6
    see also houseguests
the home see the bathroom; house
    and garden; house rules; the
    kitchen; the toilet
home brands 302
home cinemas 4
horn use, when driving 121
hot chips, in the office 67
hot-desking 64
hot food 583
hotels, appliances in 505
house and garden 494–9
house rules 2–9
houseguests 413–16
'hubby', avoiding the use of 570
humour, sense of 72, 638
hunting, as a sport 493

ice cream makers 545
inspiration see advice and inspiration
Instagram see social media
instructional YouTube videos 340
internet commenting 341–9
introductions 636, 637
invitations 365, 386, 561
iPad styluses 512
iPads 517, 521
'it is what it is' 29

jam, in plastic packets 161
jargon, in zoom meetings 613
jeans 251, 253

jewellery, on men 176
jokes 61, 158, 166, 620

the kitchen 21–5, 288
kitchen sinks 21
Kmart 547

ladders, age limits for 520
language 71–89
    'ass' versus 'arse' 572
    avoiding devaluing words 565
    avoiding inappropriate analogies
        227
    avoiding 'optics' 566
    avoiding the phrase 'happy wife,
        happy life' 192
    avoiding the phrase 'Okay Boomer'
        510
    avoiding the word 'hubby' 570
    avoiding the word 'lover' 186
    'being intimate' with someone 206
    curbing the use of Americanisms
        571
    for dogs 237
    'invite' as a noun 386
    'medal' and 'podium' as verbs 563
    on social media 332
    speaking 'to' things 564
    using jargon in zoom meetings 613
    using the right pronoun 531
    using the term 'going viral' 333
    'versing' someone 562
    see also conversation
leather pants 255
leggings 33, 37
leisure and lifestyle 489–93
lettuce 133, 549
libraries, talking in 433
life coaches 30
'like', in conversation 87
listening, in conversation 90
litter trays 240
lockdowns 541, 644–5
long hair, on old men 44
love shows 436–9, 607

luggage carousels, at airports 112
luggage, wearing of 506
lunch breaks 66, 168

maiden names 637
makeup 268–71, 490
mascara 490
masks, in the pandemic 573–9
'medal', as a verb 563
media rooms 4
meeting and greeting 632–7
meetings 68, 611–24
memes 523
microwave ovens 587
Millennials 523, 525–8
mirrors, in old age 52
mobile phones 310–22
    calling friends from your car 603
    eating while on the phone 581
    in the cinema 278
    on silent in the office 56
    on the toilet 20
    personal calls in the office 62
    putting children on to 'say hello' 215
    sending memes to Millennials 523
    stating your whereabouts when on
        631
    taking calls when with your partner
        193
    versus zoom meetings 611
    when ordering in a cafe 555
    see also texting
models 273
mothers 211, 223–9, 402
movie-makers, guidelines for 285–92
the movies 274–92, 584
    see also movie-makers; popcorn
moving footways 109
museums and art galleries 419–24
muting, in zoom meetings 623

natural history museums 419
New Year's Eve 405–6
news, podcasts as 601
'nom-noms' 84

non-drinkers 154
nose-picking 191

the office 54–70, 353
    see also email
online dating, for men 196–8
online dating, for women 199–200
oranges, cutting up of 173
outdoor wear 248

the pandemic 535–42, 573–9, 642–5
panic-buying 536
parenting 207–17
    cutting parents some slack 532
    enticing children out of the bedroom
        530
    parents at children's parties 561
    see also children; children's parties;
        fathers; mothers
parks, working out in 43
parties and celebrations 230–3,
    364–407
    see also birthdays; dinner parties;
        Halloween; weddings
'pashing' 51
pass the parcel 233
pedestrians, use of courtesy waves by
    115
penises 54–5, 396
performers, friends of 608–9
perfume, on first dates 175
pet names 185
pets 234–40, 629–31
phones see mobile phones
photographs
    family photos 5
    glamour photos 9
    in Airbnbs 500
    on dating profiles 198, 199
    pregnancy photos 218
    showing photos of your kids on first
        dates 179
    swiping through someone else's
        photos 316

photographs *continued*
  taking photos of famous paintings 421
  using iPads to take 521
  wedding photos 390–2
  with Santa 404
picnics, food for 595
piercings 263, 264
pillow fights, in movies 287
pizza leftovers 587
planes *see* flying
podcasts 596–603
'podium', as a verb 563
poke bowls 134
poncewobbling 86
popcorn 281–4
potato chips 584
prams, in cafes 211
pregnancy 218–22
presents, at weddings 382
pronouns 531
proposing, in public 188–9
public speaking 27
public transport 122–7

QR codes 542
quiet carriages 126

reading landings 443
reality television 434–46, 604–7
recipe bloggers 338
recipe websites 591–4
red velvet cake 594
relationships and dating 175–206
religion, in conversation 96
renovation shows 440–3
reply-all button 57
restaurants *see* cafes and restaurants
retailers 546–8, 578
reverse parking 120
rules, agreeing with 1

salads 554
salt, communal 159
salting, of meals 137

sandwiches 595
Santa, photographs with 404
scooching, at security checks 113
security checks, at airports 113
self-service checkouts 302–3
sex 201–6, 638–41
  Generation Z sleepovers 533–4
  in aeroplane toilets 106
  special rules for footballers 361, 363
sex therapists 203
shoes 243, 244, 246
shop assistants 293–7, 324, 578
shopping 543–8
  see also change rooms (in clothes
    shops); shop assistants;
    supermarkets
sick days 526–7
signs, in the office 61
singing 47, 70
single-use appliances 545
sleepovers 533–4
sleigh beds 499
smash cakes 232
smelly food, in the office 66, 67
smoking 31–2
sniffing passengers, on planes 107
snoring passengers, on planes 105
social media 326–34
  avoiding when 'sick' 527
  Facebook birthday greetings 369
  TikTok as a job 529
  vaccine information on 514
social zooms 624
socialising 624–8, 632–6
  see also friends
socks 244, 245
soft furnishings, life advice on 26
sound systems 3
sous vide machines 545
spiralisers 585
sport 350–63, 491–3
storytelling 515, 524
styluses, for iPads 512
sunglasses 265–7

supermarkets 298–304, 537, 538
surround sound 3

takeaway coffees 551
talking, on the toilet 16
tattoos 256–62
team-bonding activities 60
technology *see* blogging; email;
    instructional YouTube videos;
    internet commenting; mobile
    phones; social media
teenagers, things to avoid asking 569
televisions 494–5
texting
    by Baby Boomers 522
    cancelling an event by 364
    e-cards 559
    saying thank you for free tickets by
        609
    silent texting 314
    using abbreviations 557
    versus voicemail 322
    walking while texting 312
    when someone dies 558
    wishing someone happy birthday by
        368
the theatre, leaving at interval 428
thongs 246
TikTok 529
tips 166
toasted sandwiches 549
the toilet
    checking after flushing 19
    food and beverages in 17
    on planes 102, 106
    phone calls on 20
    shutting the door 15
    signs in the office toilet 61
    talking on 16
toilet rolls 13–14, 537
tomatoes, in guacamole 129
toothbrushing 574
touching, when socialising 633

towels 417, 502
trains and trams *see* public transport
travel *see* holidays and travel
'tribe', referring to your 83
TVs 494–5
twin basins 11

underpants 509

vaccines, information about 514
vaping 32
vegans, at dinner parties 375–6
Vegemite 418
vegetarians 95, 155, 553
'versing' 562
voicemail 322

waitstaff
    being polite to 150
    flirting with 49
    inappropriate use of 152
    writing down orders 156
water 136, 162
water features 496
weddings 381–99
weight lifting 38
'wellness', as a word 81
white furniture, in Airbnbs 504
women footballers 492
words *see* language
work, turning up for 526
working out 38–43
    see also change rooms (in gyms);
        exercise gear

yoga 328
yoga pants 489
youth, language rules for 87–9
YouTube videos 340

zoom gigs 610
zoom meetings 611–24
zoos 425–7

488 ~~12~~ RULES

FOR LIFE

THE THANKLESS ART OF BEING CORRECT

REBECCA BANA

ABOUT THE AUTHOR

Kitty Flanagan is one of Australia's best-known comedians. She appears on TV occasionally but spends most of her time touring the country doing stand-up.

She has two dogs, one cat and a dishwasher that she loves more than all of her pets combined. Her favourite food is soup. *488 Rules for Life* is her second book.

Also by Kitty Flanagan

Bridge Burning & other hobbies—
a collection of funny true stories

488 ~~12~~ RULES FOR LIFE

THE THANKLESS ART OF BEING CORRECT

KITTY FLANAGAN

with fellow rule-makers
Sophie Braham Penny Flanagan
Adam Rozenbachs

Illustrations by Tohby Riddle

ALLEN&UNWIN
SYDNEY·MELBOURNE·AUCKLAND·LONDON

Neither the author nor the publisher has any connection with either Jordan Peterson, the author of *12 Rules for Life*, or the publisher of that book, and readers must not interpret anything in this book as giving rise to any such connection

First published in 2019

Allen & Unwin
83 Alexander Street
Crows Nest NSW 2065
Australia
Phone: (61 2) 8425 0100
Email: info@allenandunwin.com
Web: www.allenandunwin.com

 A catalogue record for this book is available from the National Library of Australia

ISBN 978 1 76087 530 5

Internal design and illustrations by Tohby Riddle
Set in 10.8/18.1 pt Interstate by Bookhouse, Sydney
Printed and bound in Australia by Griffin Press, part of Ovato

10 9 8 7 6 5 4 3 2 1 20 19 18 17 16

 The paper in this book is FSC® certified. FSC® promotes environmentally responsible, socially beneficial and economically viable management of the world's forests.

For Marmee

Contents

A word from the author   xiii

How to use this book   xv

THE FUNDAMENTAL RULE   1

AROUND THE HOME   5

General house rules   7

The bathroom   10

The kitchen   14

HEALTH & LIFESTYLE   17

A word about wellness   19

Inspiration and advice   21

Smoking   23

Exercise gear   24

Working out   26

Ageing gracefully   28

AT THE OFFICE   33

A word about open-plan offices   35

General office rules   37

Food in the office   43

LANGUAGE 47

General language rules 49

A word about the generation gap 55

Kids today 58

Conversation 60

PLANES, TRAINS & AUTOMOBILES 65

A word about air travel 67

Flying 68

SPECIAL SEALED SECTION—SCOOCHING 75

On the road 78

Public transport 82

FOOD 85

General food rules 87

Eating 91

Dining out 95

Cafes and restaurants 97

SPECIAL SEALED SECTION—FRUIT 103

RELATIONSHIPS & DATING 109

A word about mixed messages 111

First date don'ts 115

Couples 118

Friends of couples 123

Online dating rules—for men 124

Online dating rules—for women 127

Sex 128

PARENTING   131

A word about the parenting expert   133

General parenting rules   134

Pregnancy   140

SPECIAL SEALED SECTION—FOR MUMS   143

Children's parties   147

Pets   149

FASHION   153

A word about fashion   155

General fashion rules   157

Fashion for the over-forties   160

Denim and leather   162

SPECIAL SEALED SECTION—TATTOOS   163

Piercings and other holes   167

Sunglasses   168

Makeup   169

Models   172

AT THE MOVIES   173

A word about the cinema   175

For movie-goers   177

SPECIAL SEALED SECTION—POPCORN   181

A word about Gold Class cinema   185

For movie-makers   188

AT THE SHOPS   193

A word about Sunday trading   195

Shop assistants   197

Attention, supermarket shoppers   200

Big supermarkets   201

SPECIAL SEALED SECTION—CHANGE ROOMS   203

TECHNOLOGY   207

A word about our own importance   209

Mobile phones   210

Email   214

Social media   215

Blogging   219

Instructional YouTube videos   222

Internet commenting   224

SPORT   229

A word about sport   231

For sports fans   233

For non-enthusiasts   235

Special rules for footballers   237

PARTIES & CELEBRATIONS   239

A word about parties   241

Invitations and attendance   242

Birthdays   244

Dinner parties   245

Weddings   250

SPECIAL SEALED SECTION—WEDDING SPEECHES 255

Halloween 259

Xmas, New Year's Eve and the other one 261

HOLIDAYS & TRAVEL 263

Australians overseas 265

A word about bunking in 267

Houseguests 270

Visitors to our shores 272

ART & ENTERTAINMENT 273

A word about 'culture' 275

Museums and art galleries 277

The zoo 281

The theatre 284

Books 285

SPECIAL REMOVABLE SECTION—
REALITY TELEVISION 287

THE FINAL RULE 295

Acknowledgements 303

A word from the author

This book started out as a five-minute segment on ABC TV's *The Weekly* program, it was inspired by the bestselling book *12 Rules for Life* and it was a joke. I took issue with the fact that author, Jordan Peterson, only had twelve rules. Twelve? For life? That's madness, I have more than twelve rules just for the bathroom.

After the segment aired, I kept being stopped by people wanting to know where they could buy this book (that didn't actually exist) called *488 Rules for Life*. It was suddenly apparent that I wasn't the only crackpot out there who loves rules. So I decided to do the book for real. But it's still a joke. Even I admit that 488 is a lot of rules and obviously no one will like all of the rules, but I'm pretty sure everyone will like *some* of the rules. And when you do hit a particular rule that resonates, it will make you feel really good—you'll enjoy the fact that someone else gets as annoyed or outraged or exhausted by the same things you do.

If, by some chance, you manage to read the entire book and don't find a single rule you agree with and instead keep thinking, *I don't get why she's so irritated by people? Why can't she just live and let live?* that's okay, that's your prerogative . . . as long as you understand you are probably really annoying a lot of people around you with your unbearable positivity and your 'I love everything' attitude.

I think, deep down, people are crying out for rules. Once it was commonplace to look to published guides for advice on behaviour, protocol and etiquette. Guides produced by recognised authorities, such as *Debrett's* in the United Kingdom and Emily Post in the United States. Even in Australia we had our very own Miss Manners, the formidable June Dally-Watkins— I met her once, she didn't say hello, she just looked me up and down and told me in no uncertain terms I should never wear a white bra under a white shirt. 'Always nude, dear, always nude.'

But these days there is no such guide in circulation, and I believe the rise in rude behaviour and the lack of basic courtesy we are witnessing in the modern world is quite possibly due to ignorance. If you don't know the rules, how are you supposed to abide by them?

Which is why I say, thank god for me. Now, with this comprehensive reference book at your fingertips, there can be no excuse for bad behaviour. Whenever you're unsure about the right way to behave, whenever you want to know what *not* to do in any given situation, simply turn to *488 Rules for Life*. The answer is bound to be in here somewhere.

How to use this book

This book is divided into sections and within each section you will find a range of rules. Some are fairly basic, things that everyone should already know; others are more specific and are for the people I call genuine rule enthusiasts. And occasionally you will come across rules so particular and persnickety that only absolute zealots like myself will be able to get on board. I have separated these into special sealed sections so that the more tolerant reader can avoid them easily.

Whatever level of rule disciple you are, know that reading this book and observing these rules will definitely make the world a nicer place. I also guarantee you will be better looking and better informed; in fact, you'll be a better human overall. So think of it as a self-help book, only you don't have to give up sugar, buy expensive exercise equipment or keep a diary of your dreams. All you have to do is speak up when you see someone breaking the rules. A gentle but friendly reminder is all it takes: 'Hey buddy! Rule number 266—no sunglasses on the back of your neck, cheers mate, just letting you know.' There's no need to be rude or confrontational about it, keep it light—remember, like me, you're here to help.

THE FUNDAMENTAL RULE

1
If you don't agree with a rule, forget about it, move on to the next one

Whatever you do, don't get angry and start bleating on social media about how it would be impossible to live your life by these 488 rules. That's not what this book is about.

AROUND THE HOME

GENERAL HOUSE RULES

2
Football jerseys are not art

Don't frame them. And definitely don't hang them on the wall.

3
Don't waste your money on surround sound

Nobody cares, guys. And I say guys because it is usually guys who insist on surround sound. When I'm watching TV, I find it weird if the sound isn't coming from the television. After all, the person walking on the television is *on the television*, in front of me, so it's really creepy to hear footsteps behind me or, indeed, all around me.

Same goes for those elaborate sound systems that people (again, usually men) install. The ones where they wire up the entire house with speakers in every room so they can pipe their chunes throughout. It's not a department store, it's just your house, you don't need the music to follow you around wherever you go. Spend your money on nice ham instead.

4
You don't need a media room or home cinema

Just watch television in the lounge room like a normal person. Or go to the cinema.

5
Supersizing is for beverages not family portraits

There are many businesses that will blow up your family photo onto an enormous canvas, but that doesn't mean you should get one. A few regular-sized photos will do just fine; you don't want to turn your living room into some kind of in-memoriam shrine.

6
Don't complain about your cleaner

Having a cleaner is one of life's greatest luxuries and if you can afford one you should be extremely grateful. And no matter how lax you might think your cleaner is, remember, it's still better than mopping your own kitchen floor or scrubbing your own bathroom and pulling your own disgusting hair-monster out of the plughole.

7
Wait a week before accusing your cleaner of stealing

People always accuse the cleaner. Never to their face but behind their back in hushed tones to their friends: 'I think the cleaner might have taken my necklace/favourite plate/earring/five bucks/tape measure/spatula, etc.'

Your cleaner is not stupid, cleaners know they will always be number one on the suspect list, which is why I guarantee the cleaner did not take your stuff.

Here's the more likely scenario: you've put your necklace/favourite plate/earring/five bucks/tape measure/spatula some-where you don't usually put it and then done what all middle-aged people do—completely forgotten where you put it.

Give it a week; whatever the cleaner has 'stolen' will turn up.

8
Flags are not curtains

A flag in the window is a tell-tale sign that backpackers have moved in. And if the NSW tourism department is at all interested in my amateur research, I would say that based on the number of flag curtains in my area, the majority of visitors to Bondi Junction are coming from Ireland and Brazil. Welcome to you all . . . now please go buy some curtains.

9
Glamour shots belong in a drawer

First, think very carefully about whether you really need a soft-focus, glassy-eyed shot of yourself dressed in high heels and a feather boa, kneeling on a whorish-looking bed surrounded by red satin cushions. And then think even more carefully about whether you need to put that photo on display anywhere.

THE BATHROOM

10
Your bathroom must have a door

This sounds absurdly obvious but there is a disturbing trend among fancy-pants architects at the moment to create en suite bathrooms with glass doors, or worse, *no* doors. I understand the desire to merge your indoor and outdoor spaces or to combine your living and dining room, but this open-plan bedroom-bathroom thing is nothing more than a seamless merger of pretension and gross impracticality (emphasis on the gross).

11
One basin is ample

No matter how much you and your partner love doing stuff together, there is absolutely no need to brush your teeth standing side by side, each with your own individual basin. Personally, I prefer to be alone in the bathroom no matter what I'm doing. However, if you happen to be one of those weird couples who like being in the bathroom together, abluting at the same time, then surely you are comfortable enough to spit into the same sink. Which means 'twin vanities' are completely unnecessary. One bathroom, one basin.

12
Don't marinate in your own filth

The bathroom is not a library, there are far more pleasant, not to mention less smelly, places to read your book. Don't linger in there, get in get out.

13
Replace the toilet roll

Just do it. You're a grown-up. It takes ten seconds.

14
Do not leave one square of toilet paper on the roll

Don't kid yourself, this is worse than not replacing the roll because of the effort required to leave that one square behind. Everyone knows it wasn't an accident, it was a carefully orchestrated event carried out in order to avoid replacing the roll. You pulled gently on the paper, taking great care not to unravel all of it and leave an empty roll. You may even have reverse-rolled it to make sure you left that one square on there: one square that you know perfectly well is of no use to anyone.

And don't be the dick that just sits the new roll on top of the empty roll, that doesn't count either.

15
Shut the bathroom door

I'll brook no argument or discussion about this one. If you are on the toilet, shut the bathroom door; it's a basic courtesy to your fellow householders. No one should have to see anyone else mid-evacuation with their pants around their ankles. Parents with small children, you are the exception. I realise that toddlers like to be able to access you at all times and will often hammer relentlessly on a closed bathroom door, concerned and some-times even alarmed about your sudden disappearance from view. (My dog is a bit the same.)

16
No talking on the toilet

The only words you should ever have to utter while on the toilet are 'I'm in here' or 'just a minute' in response to an enquiring knock on the door. Nothing is so important that it can't wait until you exit the bathroom. This rule is of particular concern in public bathrooms. A lot of women love a gabfest in the can, somehow forgetting that there are germs flying around all over the place, and by flapping your gums and having a good old chitty chat, you are inviting those germs right into your mouth. Bottom line, if your bum is open, your mouth should be closed.

17
Don't take food or beverages into the toilet

Who'd have thought that ever needed to be said? But apparently it does. You know who you are (American guy called Tom who lives in Manchester) and whom I witnessed take a newspaper and 'hot cup of joe' into the bathroom.

18
The bathroom bin is for bathroom rubbish only

Sometimes you find that the bathroom bin is the closest bin. Perhaps you arrive home, you've just finished eating a banana or a packet of Twisties and you spy the bathroom bin as you walk down the hall. You must forgo the urge to toss your empty wrappers in there. Because what happens is, the next time someone is using the toilet, they'll look down into the bin, see the banana skin and think, *Oh dear god, was someone eating a banana on the can? How disgusting!*

19
Flush. Pause. Check—FPC

Always wait after flushing so you can do a final check to make sure you are leaving nothing behind. Nothing. Not a mark, not a smear—there should be zero evidence of what's gone on in that bathroom. Don't leave a crime scene.

20
No phone calls on the toilet

The only thing worse than having a phone call with someone who is on the toilet is the realisation that they are indeed on the toilet. It's usually something that dawns on you slowly. Probably because—for most normal people—the idea of making calls from the dunny is beyond comprehension, so it always takes a while to put all the pieces together. First you notice the strange echo-chamber effect, then come the oddly timed pauses and strangled grunts in their speech. 'So I wondered if you . . . *hnnnn* . . . could let Margaret . . . *hnnnnnnn* . . . know that I might be late . . . *hnn* . . . today.' And finally confirmation comes when you actually hear the waterfall cascading into the bowl or, worse, the splashdown. Unbelievable as it may seem, a lot of people take calls while on the toilet; I know because I hear them do it in public toilets all the time. A phone rings and then the person actually answers it? 'Yeah . . . *hnnny*hello?' What is wrong with these people? The toilet cubicle is not a phone booth.

THE KITCHEN

21
The sink is not a dishwasher

These days most people have a dishwasher or, as I like to call it, a magic, electric, washy-washy box. And it really is magical, you can put anything in there and it comes out clean, requiring minimal effort on your part. Yet there are still people who think that dumping dishes in the sink, near the dishwasher, is good enough. It isn't. Either go the extra half a yard (literally—the dishwasher is never far from the sink) and pop that sucker in the dishwasher *or* wash it up. They're your two options. Do not, however, just plonk it in the sink and think, *Well done me!*

22
Everything can go in the dishwasher

Everything. No matter how big. Even if it takes ten minutes to rearrange everything in order to cram that saucepan or wok or blender jug in there, it's better than having to spend two minutes washing something up.

23
Flog the dishwasher until it does the job properly

Sometimes the dishwasher does a half-arsed job and you find something that still has a bit of food stuck to it. When that happens, it's up to the dishwasher to make things right. Don't be a martyr and clean the dish or frying pan or wooden spoon your-self—that's rewarding the dishwasher for shoddy workmanship. Instead, you put whatever it is right back in the dishwasher and leave it there until it comes out clean. Whether it takes another two or another twenty wash cycles, it doesn't matter: the dishwasher has got to learn.

24
One person cooks, the other cleans up

In a couple or a family, the person who cooks the meal should never have to clean up as well. If you live alone, obviously this is not feasible, therefore I suggest you try to cook as neatly as you can. However, I must stress that this 'cook neatly' thing is a guideline, or recommendation, not a rule. As someone who lives alone and cooks like the Swedish chef from *The Muppets*, I cannot in all good conscience instruct anyone to 'clean as you go'.

25
Clean up the kitchen before you go to bed

Again, not really a rule, more of a note to self.

HEALTH & LIFESTYLE

A word about wellness

Wellness advocates and experts all claim they can improve your quality of life, whether it's by not eating sugar or by drawing toxins out of your body with hot cups and candles or by rubbing your face with dung because that's what some tribe did 5000 years ago in a tiny part of outer Mongolia. But sometimes I think we can get distracted by all the hype and forget to look at the bigger picture.

I was backstage at a corporate event once and witnessed a well-known anti-sugar crusader nibbling the dark chocolate coating off a single almond. She was scraping it off in tiny bits with her front teeth. It took her about twenty minutes. She noticed me staring (it was hard to look away, she was gnawing at that thing like a rat on a cable) and confessed that she allowed herself a minuscule amount of dark chocolate every day as her little reward. I told her quite smugly that I didn't allow myself

any dark chocolate whatsoever. I didn't say that it was because dark chocolate is a punishment disguised as confectionery, rather I just enjoyed pretending I took my health more seriously than she did.

I know she looks better than me and I know she'll live longer than me, but my point about looking at the bigger picture is that I'm not sure I want to live longer if the only 'treat' I'm allowed is one dark chocolate nut per day. Especially if I have to eat it hunched over in a corner like an obsessive-compulsive squirrel.

And for the record, I don't want to drink bone broth for breakfast or rub my face with dung either. I guess I just don't care enough about my own wellness—which is not a word, by the way—and you can read more about that in Language Rules.

INSPIRATION AND ADVICE

26
Cushions are not spiritual advisors

The current trend for putting trite advice on soft furnishings has to stop. No one has ever read *Live, Love, Laugh* on a pillow or *Dream, Relax, Feel* on a wall hanging and thought, *Oh what an excellent idea, I've not lived, loved or laughed in ages. Well, that all changes right now, thank you, cushion!*

In fact, more often than not, I find these clichéd bon mots have the opposite effect and actually inspire rage and the desire to punch something, usually a cushion with the hateful *Keep Calm and Carry On* printed on it.

27
Never tell someone to 'just imagine the audience naked'

This is one of the dumbest things you can ever say to a person who is about to do a bit of public speaking. There would be nothing more distracting than looking around a room and imagining what everyone looks like in the nude. How are you supposed to remember your speech when you're envisaging a room full of lumpy naked people?

28
Don't offer up clichés as advice

No one who has just been dumped wants to hear, 'There are plenty more fish in the sea.' It means nothing. If you must trot out this hoary old chestnut, then at least try to make it more accurate. 'There are plenty more fish in the sea ... *but* there are also a lot of bottom feeders and unpleasant smelly creatures that won't be to your taste at all, plus a few nasty aggressive types with big sharp teeth, so maybe the ocean's not the best place to go looking for a new partner.'

29
'It is what it is' actually means 'please stop talking'

When someone says, 'It is what it is', they are not being wise and philosophical, rather they are sick of listening to you and are trying to wrap up the conversation.

30
Life is not a sport so you don't need a coach

When life coaches first hit the scene, which I think was back in the nineties, it seemed like they were some kind of southern Californian joke that would go away faster than the trend for walking with ski stocks or using a PalmPilot organiser.

Life coaches, however, have not gone away, they have proliferated. And what has become apparent over the years is that, oftentimes, life coaches are people who have failed at other professions. So really the only advice a life coach should be doling out is: 'If you want to turn your life around and become successful, you should become a life coach. Because then you can get paid to tell someone else how to turn their life around and become successful . . . by becoming a life coach.'

Come to think of it, maybe that's exactly what they are doing and maybe that's why there are so many life coaches out there.

SMOKING

31
If you smoke, you smell

All the time. And that's okay, as long as you are aware of it. Sucking a mint only makes you smell like a smoker who has just sucked a mint. And washing your hands makes you smell like a smoker who has just washed their hands. Again, that's fine, just don't think you're fooling anyone.

32
If you vape, you look a lot less cool than you think

In fact, you look like you are blowing a USB stick. Or R2-D2's detachable penis.

EXERCISE GEAR

33
Only buy black leggings

Any other colour simply makes a feature of the sweat around your box and crack. Pop on a pair of light grey leggings next time you exercise and you'll see that even when you barely break a sweat up top, downstairs you'll be showcasing a right Rorschach inkblot test in your pants. That's why people in the gym are staring— they're either trying to work out what the stain resembles or, worse, they're wondering if you've wet yourself. Because it's difficult to tell the difference between sweat and wee, so there's a good chance you'll just look like a lady who went a bit too wide on her warrior pose and blew a piss-valve.

34
Stop calling it active wear

Most people I see wearing 'active wear' are at the shopping centre. So perhaps we should use the term 'Lycra shopping outfit' instead.

35
Once you are no longer active, get changed

You may wear your exercise gear en route to the gym or the park or the hot yoga dojo or wherever you are going to be active. You may also keep it on as you make your way home again and you may even detour to the shops, briefly, to pick up a couple of things. But that's it. Once you're home, admit that you're not going to be doing any more lunges or downward dogs and that it's time to put on some less-active wear.

36

Dress according to the standard of cyclist you are

Many of us enjoy a hit of tennis yet I never see anyone down at my local club sporting a full Serena Williams-style catsuit. Cyclists should bear that in mind and rethink their cycling gear. If you're not racing in the Tour de France, there's absolutely no need for those gut-hugging tops with multiple pockets all around that allow you to strap energy bars to yourself like dynamite on a suicide bomber vest.

You can probably live without those three bananas and four Clif Bars, not to mention the numerous electrolyte sachets. After all, you're only going to be riding for about an hour at the most. The larger part of your morning will be spent sprawled across multiple tables at the local cafe drinking lattes with all the other middle-aged men in padded ball-bag pants and zip tops covered in logos of sponsors who aren't actually your sponsors. And the reason they aren't your sponsors is because you're not a professional cycling team. You're just some dads in clip-cloppy shoes trying to get out of parenting on a Sunday morning.

37

Men must wear shorts over leggings

The gym is no place for people to discover whether or not you are circumcised. That's a private discussion for another place and time.

WORKING OUT

38
Lift less, more quietly

The odd noise of exertion here and there is fine, but if you are grunting and puffing and blowing your cheeks out to the point where bits of spit are starting to fly around, take some weight off, it's obviously too much for you.

39
Don't tell people you box

You participate in a boxing class. It's different.

40
No naked parading in the change rooms

I don't care how good your body is, I don't want to see it striding from one end of the change room to the other, or bending over while you rummage around in your gym bag for your matching bra and lacy thong set. You have a towel, use it.

41
No vigorous towelling

Pat or blot yourself dry after a shower. Don't rub yourself so hard that all your bits start wobbling and jiggling about. Just accept that it may not be possible to get yourself bone dry when you're in a communal change area—that's why talcum powder was invented. Channel your inner old lady and throw a bit of powdery talc around down there instead.

42

Keep two feet firmly planted on the ground at all times

Under no circumstances should you treat the change room like a woodchopping event. Don't even think about putting one foot up on the bench and then using that towel like a two-handed saw, going back and forth between your legs. If that's how you must dry yourself, wait for an individual cubicle to become available and have a go at yourself in private.

43

The park is not a gym

Take your kettle bells, your giant ropes and your lumpy male trainers shouting, 'Don't give up on me, Doyanne! (Dianne)' and get out of what should be a lovely green space in which to relax, perambulate, picnic or just play on the swings. (If you're a child that is—please don't be one of those cutesy girl-women who giggles and gets her date to push her on the swing in a bid to be adorable.)

AGEING GRACEFULLY

44
Old men should not have long hair

Cut the ponytail off, fellas. The bad news is, it probably wasn't even cool way back when you were young, but now it's even less cool *and* it's making everyone around you a bit sad.

45
Don't lie about your age

The number one thing to remember about getting older (aside from the fact that old men shouldn't have long hair) is that lying about your age is pointless. If you try to appear younger by knocking a few years off when you state your age, all anyone thinks is, *Wow, she looks dreadful!* or *Does this old bat think I'm stupid?*

When someone asks me how old I am, I prefer to add a few years rather than take them off. That way people will think, *Gee, she looks pretty damn good for sixty-five!* However, this trick doesn't always go to plan. The inherent and ever-present danger is that when you tell someone you're sixty-five and you're really only forty-five, they may simply take you at your word and think, *Yeah, that seems about right.*

46
Put your feet away

Nothing gives away your age faster than cracked white heels and gnarly, split, yellow toenails. There is an odd phenomenon that occurs when men retire—for some reason they refuse to wear shoes anymore and instead decide to live out the rest of their lives in sandals. It's like suddenly they want everyone to bear witness to the hideous crime scene they have going on at the end of each ankle.

When I hit retirement age, I plan to petition the government for a pensioner pedicure subsidy for both men and women. A weekly pedicure for the elderly is a great idea. For a start it prevents an old person's feet from turning into a pair of festering petri-dish experiments, but more importantly, it provides a much-needed social outing for lonely seniors. After all, the manicurist is the perfect captive audience, trapped at the business end of the pedicure chair while the old person chatters away.

47
Don't start singing like a Bee Gee

If you are having trouble hitting all the notes in your regular singing voice due to age, taking it up a notch and trying to sing in the key of 'old lady falsetto' isn't going to help. Just turn your volume down and drone along quietly instead.

48
No one wants to hear about your ailments

That doesn't mean you have to stop talking about them, just be aware that there is not a person in the world who is interested, not even friends the same age as you. The only reason they willingly listen to you talk about your various afflictions is so they can rabbit on about their *own* ailments the minute your mouth stops moving. It's a bore exchange.

49
Leave the waitstaff alone

Flirting with waiters half your age is unseemly and could also be viewed as a mild form of solicitation—because waiters will always be polite and often times flirt right back—but it's only because they want a tip. Ergo, you're only getting their attention because you're paying for it.

Men, no matter what age they are, flirt with waitstaff. They do it when they're young and they keep doing it when they get old. And they always think they're being incredibly charming. They're not. For women, however, flirting with waitstaff is only something they tend to take up with enthusiasm once they hit middle age. It's like they've finally found their confidence and suddenly they think it's a bit cheeky and hilarious to hit on fit, young waiters. But it isn't. For while the woman may see herself as a real cougar, all the waiter sees is a mangy old housecat yowling for attention.

50
Don't pretend you don't need glasses

If you're holding the menu at arm's length, you need glasses. If the font on your phone is billboard-sized and can be read by someone at the other end of the train carriage, you *really* need glasses.

51
Don't use the word 'pash' anymore

Once you are forty, the time for pashing is well past. You can still do it if you must, but please find another word to describe it.

52
Have a mirror right next to the front door

You might not want to look at your ageing self but remember, a mirror is your best friend. And having a mirror right next to the front door, preferably a magnifying mirror, should be mandatory for all people aged forty-five and over. Basically, you want to do a quick check before you leave the house. You're looking for renegade hairs and they could be anywhere: upper lip and chin for ladies; ears and nose (inside and out) if you're a man. You want to remove anything that would transfix a small child and have them reaching out to tug it.

You also need to keep an eye out for those random straggly eyebrows that are so long you can only assume they've been growing out of your face since birth. How else do you explain the absurd length of them?

Once you're happy you're not leaving the house looking like the missing link, then do a quick once-over of your clothes, checking for any food spills. At a certain age, having a food stain down your front is the equivalent of having a sign around your neck that reads, *They're going to put me in a home soon.*

53
Men, don't dye your hair

For some reason, it just doesn't work for you. And most of you look pretty good grey anyway. Which, personally, I find quite annoying. Men with grey hair are always described as 'silver foxes'—people use words like 'sophisticated' or 'Clooney-esque'. Whereas when I allow my hair to go grey, the only celebrity I resemble is Meryl Streep in *Into the Woods*.

AT THE OFFICE

A word about open-plan offices

It has been a long time since I've had a 'real' job and worked full time in a 'real' office. My most recent in-office experience was at the ABC during the production of the show that spawned this book, The Weekly with Charlie Pickering. *In Melbourne, the ABC offices are housed in a brand-new, shiny building in Southbank. It cost a lot of money and I guess they spent most of that money on the outside of the building, which is why they didn't have enough cash left to pay for any walls inside the building, walls that would help divide the vast open spaces into individual offices for people to work in. I can think of no other reason, other than budget, that would explain why our national broadcaster would inflict one of the most universally reviled working arrangements on their underpaid, overworked and yet surprisingly dedicated and loyal staff. Pretty much the whole of the ABC is open plan. Well, except where the executives work—that part of the office* got walls **and** doors, which the execs must find really annoying. After all, they're the ones who constantly champion open plan and tell the rest of us how great it is.

When I arrived at the ABC and discovered The Weekly office was open plan, I decided to work from home. This was not an arrangement I came to with management; rather, it was the only way I could get any work done. I never told anyone I was working from home, instead, I came in every morning, put my jacket on the back of my chair, scattered a few notes across my desk, placed my bag underneath, then took what I needed and went home to do some work. I was able to get away with this because at the time I lived only ten minutes down the road. So if I got a text or a call saying, 'Where are you?' or 'Can you come to the meeting room for a read-through?' I would reply, 'Sure, just grabbing a coffee, back in ten. Smiley face emoji, coffee cup emoji, heart emoji, two exclamation marks.'

Ultimately, I was far more productive working from home than I would have been sitting out in the open among thirty other employees, a lot of whom were making necessary but still very distracting phone calls and some of whom were making distracting and completely unnecessary phone calls.

It did mean there was a fair bit of driving back and forth — which gives rise to my argument that the open-plan office model is not only highly unproductive thanks to the miserable employees it creates, but in my case it also contributed to global warming because of the time I spent on the road burning fossil fuels.

GENERAL OFFICE RULES

54
Don't take your wang out at the office, ever

I realise this seems incredibly obvious but in the current climate, with everything that's come to light about men sending dick pics, wanking in front of female colleagues or into pot plants, and showing off their knobs to co-workers like you would a new iPhone etc., apparently we do need to spell this one out. So here it is again:

55
Your penis should remain in your pants during office hours

Unless you are ALONE in a toilet cubicle using it to wee—then it can come out—but please, put it away as soon as you're done.

56
During office hours, turn your phone to silent

It's common courtesy; no one in the office wants to hear your Bernard Fanning, 'I Just Want to Wish You Well' ringtone, in full, every time your phone rings. No one. Not even Bernard.

57
Go easy on the reply-all button

We all get enough rubbish filling up our inboxes, we certainly don't need to be included in irrelevant reply-all chains. Just because someone emailed a question to the entire office doesn't mean you have to reply-all; just reply to the person who sent the email.

58
Don't insert yay into Friday

No matter how happy you are that the week has ended, there's no need to resort to using office clichés like 'Friyay'. Especially in pointless inter-office group emails: *Happy FriYAY everyone!* Everyone knows it's Friday. Everyone knows the weekend is coming. Everyone is happy. No one's mood is buoyed by your arbitrary yaying.

'Hump Day' is similar to Friyay, in that there's never any call for it. If you can't think of anything to say to an associate in your office besides 'Happy Hump Day!' just give them a polite nod and pass without saying anything. It's not compulsory to speak every time you pass one another. See rule 63 for clarification on the correct way to greet co-workers.

59
Stop the senseless 'e-meeting'

Don't write 'pleased to e-meet you' at the top of an email. You lost me at 'e'—I'm not reading any further.

60
Team bonding activities should be optional

Some people love it when management decides that an afternoon of bowling or paintballing or (god forbid) karaoke will help everyone work better as a team. Others would rather be dead. So respect the rights of those who hate 'forced fun', which also includes themed 'dress-up days'—not everyone enjoys wearing a fascinator around the office to celebrate Melbourne Cup Day. And maybe Fay from Purchasing is self-conscious about her broad caboose and doesn't want to wear jeans on *any* day, let alone on Jeans for Genes Day when she'll feel even more conspicuous in her sheets-of-denim being compared to everyone else in their teeny-tiny skinny jeans.

61
Don't attempt humour in signs around the office

The problem with the jokey sign is that it does not withstand repeat viewings. People go to the kitchen or bathroom several times a day and there's no way your note is funny enough that folks will enjoy it and chuckle every time they see it. What you should aim for in an office note is mild terseness. You do this by employing shouty caps and underlining:

PUT YOUR DISHES IN THE DISHWASHER—PLEASE

But avoid doing 'gags' like taking a poster of a cute pussycat and writing the following underneath it:

WASH YOUR CUP OR THIS KITTEN GETS IT!

And if you need to put up signs in the bathroom, humour should be the last thing on your mind. When I visit an office and see a sign like this in the bathroom:

IF YOU SPRINKLE WHEN YOU TINKLE,
BE A SWEETIE, WIPE THE SEATIE

I'm not thinking, *Oh that's funny 'cos it rhymes*, I'm thinking, *Who in god's name is pissing on the seat so often that a sign is required?* After all, I'm in the ladies toilet. To the best of my knowledge, ladies sit down to go to the toilet and it is physically impossible to wee on the seat when you are sitting *on* that seat. If women are somehow spraying it around like tom cats in your office bathroom, the time for joking is long past, the only sign that should go up is one that says:

HEY LADIES, <u>SIT DOWN</u>

62
No personal calls in open-plan offices

In this unfortunate, modern world of open-plan offices, it surprises me that I have to articulate this as a rule. I assumed everyone was like me and got really self-conscious making personal phone calls when other people were within earshot. Turns out, some people aren't the slightest bit embarrassed about others over-hearing their personal calls, in fact they seem to revel in it. I witnessed one woman FaceTiming her young children from her open-plan office desk every day at around five o'clock. Perhaps it was her way of justifying staying late at the office. I say, if you miss your kids so much that you have to FaceTime them, just go home.

63
One proper greeting per day is ample, after that a nod will suffice

Working in an office can be stressful. Not only do you have to get your work done, you must also make an effort to socialise with your fellow employees, especially when you find yourself trapped together in the claustrophobic staff kitchen. At times it can feel as though your whole day is taken up both asking and answering bland questions like 'How was your weekend?' or 'Got anything on this weekend?' or 'Hungover much? Heh heh'.

The point is that between regular trips to the kitchen, the bathroom and even the printer (to pick up those personal documents you've been printing out at work) you will cross paths with your co-workers multiple times a day. This means multiple greetings per day, and it's not surprising that these become less enthusiastic as the day wears on. That's why it's okay to simply nod at your co-workers, or even just raise an eyebrow of acknowledgement from the second interaction onwards. It's too exhausting to have to come up with new small talk for each passing, and if you're not careful you can end up falling into the 'say what you see' trap (I am one of the worst offenders of this) passing someone in the corridor and saying something like 'Ooh, having a cup of tea' or 'Mm, chips. Good stuff'.

Others try to cover their awkwardness by attempting humour, failing, then laughing at their 'joke' anyway: 'Heyyy, nice green top, Ellen ... did you see Sophie's wearing a green top today too? Sorry guys, I didn't get the memo! Ha ha ha.'

Remember if you have nothing of substance to say, it's perfectly okay to go full Ronan Keating and say nothing at all.

64
No hot-desking

Hot-desking is a form of employee abuse. In years to come, I hope there will be a class action where all the people who have been forced to hot-desk will take their employers to court and sue them for damages. I am fortunate that I have never had to endure such torment. However, the poor staff in the ABC newsroom were long-suffering victims of hot-desking. I know they were suffering because I did an informal survey of the newsroom which revealed that no one enjoyed it. No one. Not one person said, 'Yes, I quite like not having anywhere permanent to put my things. It's also great not being able to personalise a space that I spend at least eight hours a day in. But most of all, I really like never knowing where to find anyone. It adds an element of discovery to my day.'

Incidentally, among people who are forced to hot-desk, it is much more commonly referred to as 'shit-desking'. Only management still insist on using the term 'hot-desking'. It's been proven in numerous studies, far more formal and official than mine (I just went around asking, 'On a scale of one to ten how much do you hate hot-desking?') that hot-desking does not improve employee productivity. Quite the contrary, in fact, because, while you might save money buying less furniture and office space, you lose money by having unhappy, less-efficient employees. I call Time's Up on hot-desking.

65
Comedy dancing is not dancing—just don't dance

This is a rule for all the office wags at the office Christmas party.

FOOD IN THE OFFICE

66
Don't eat at your desk

This is controversial I know, but my reason is twofold. Firstly, everyone is entitled to a lunch break. This should be an hour (or half hour) where you break and go for lunch. It's not at all cryptic. A lunch hour should not mean an hour spent at your desk with lunch in one hand, still working with the other, dropping bits of food into your keyboard and using your pants as a napkin.

Secondly, it's incredibly unhygienic to eat at your desk and it's unpleasant for your fellow workers to witness, especially if you're eating something stinky like a hard-boiled egg or something noisy like a chip sandwich. No judgement for eating a chip sandwich, by the way, that's an excellent carb on carb choice, just do it in a designated food-eating area.

67
No stinky foods in the office

Respect those around you and don't bring your leftover fish curry to work and then heat it up in the office microwave. No one wants to spend the afternoon working in the noxious fishy miasma you've just created. And while I understand that many people love tuna for its healthful and nourishing properties, I think we can all agree that it really does stink so, if you must eat it, I suggest going outside to enjoy your lunch in the open air. Don't chow down in the confines of the office where the windows only open a few inches, if at all. As for bringing hot chips into the office, that is not just smelly, it's also mean. Because for the first thirty seconds, hot chips smell delicious and now you've made everyone in the office want hot chips. However, pretty soon those hot chips will turn cold and the office will smell like every teenage McDonald's employee when they come home from a shift reeking of cold grease and congealed fat.

68
No food in meetings

We're all busy. But if you're so busy that you're bringing soup to a meeting and slurping it during proceedings, then you need to organise your day better. Either reschedule the meeting or reschedule your soup slurping.

69
Pick one day a month to do birthday cake

Office birthday cake is a minefield. Yes, cake is great but not everyone is in the mood to drop everything and suddenly gather in the conference room at some random time of day whenever it's someone's birthday. There's never a set time for birthday cake, quite often it's a case of 'Hurry up everyone, we're doing cake now because Jo is leaving early to go to a conference!' It's even less appealing when you know your only reward will be ten minutes of awkward forced togetherness and a piece of wet supermarket mud cake that you end up pushing around a paper plate with a plastic fork. I am, however, not against birthdays or cakes. My solution is to pick a day—one day a month, for argument's sake, let's say the last Friday of every month. Then on that Friday at 11 am everyone gathers in the boardroom and someone reads out a list of all the people who have celebrated a birthday that month. Cake is presented, 'Happy Birthday' is sung (in accordance with the following rule) and everyone enjoys a bit of cake for morning tea.

This allows cake to remain special, it also means everyone in the office knows when birthday cake day is approaching. You can schedule it into your workday, you can set your palate for cake, you can even stop work at 10.55 to make a cup of tea to go with your pending piece of cake. The other great advantage of this system is that it provides enough lead time for someone to actually make a decent cake. Surely that is preferable to the office junior being dispatched to Coles to procure some hideous-looking cake encased in a plastic dome every time someone reveals it's their birthday.

70
Stop singing after the final 'Happy Birthday to you'

No one wants to hear the 'For he's a jolly good fellow' extended mix featuring MC Daryl the office good-time guy on 'hip hip hoorays'. It's awkward. People have work to do. And cake to eat. Hopefully a delicious homemade one if you've adhered to the previous rule.

LANGUAGE

GENERAL LANGUAGE RULES

71
Once you hear a word used in an ad, it's time to stop using it

A good example of this would be 'hangry', which was used in a flavoured-milk ad. You don't want to use that word anymore, because if it's appeared in an ad it's officially past its use-by date. Advertising people are notorious for being one step behind and stealing ideas from other art forms, such as films, TV and comedy. I know because I used to be in advertising.

72
Never tell someone you have a GSOH

It's unnecessary. If you have a good sense of humour, it will become apparent the minute you say something funny or laugh appreciatively at something funny that someone else has said.

Similarly, you should never use the terms 'dark' or 'unique' to describe your own sense of humour. People who genuinely have a dark sense of humour don't think of it as dark, they just think of it as regular. Whereas people who *say* they have a dark or unique sense of humour are often trying to make themselves seem interesting, or justify the fact that no one laughed at something they said: 'Oh, you don't get it? Must be because I have a very dark sense of humour.'

73
Don't ever 'wonder what the poor people are doing'

It's no big mystery. They're probably thinking about where their next meal is coming from or how they're going to pay their rent.

74
Stop saying 'First World problems'

If you live in the First World, this phrase is an oxymoron. All of our problems are First World problems. So you can safely just say 'problems'. Unless, of course, you are suddenly hit with a Third World problem, then you might want to flag it as such: 'Hey?! This bowl of sorghum is tasteless and I think it's been made with polluted water, talk about Third World problems!'

Or if someone says to you: 'I can't come in to work today, I've got cholera.'

Then you can respond: 'Wow! Third World problem or what?!'

75
Clown is not a verb

It's bad enough that you are a clown, please don't try to talk it up by saying you are going to do some 'clowning' or that you learned 'to clown' in Paris.

76
Feed is not a noun

And should never be used as such, as in: 'Hey, do you want to go for a feed?' (Farmers are the obvious exception to this rule.)

77
Don't refer to your wife as 'the boss'

As in 'I'll have to check with the boss.' Apart from anything else, it's almost always disingenuous and only ever cited by men who would overrule their 'boss' in a heartbeat if she said something that didn't suit them.

78
Avoid using adjectives such as delicious or yummy in non-food contexts

For example, you can say, 'This food is delicious.' But you cannot say, 'My, my, don't you look yummy today.'

79
Don't describe inanimate objects as 'sexy'

A typeface isn't sexy. Nor is an iPhone. Home renovation show judges are flagrant in their disregard for this rule, always referring to things like tap fittings or marble bench tops or even 2PAC polycarbonate cupboards as 'sexy'.

80
Keep more ye olde words in circulation

Don't try to keep up with the youth (see next section) instead, go back in time and choose words and phrases from the past. The English language is full of great gear and it's good to keep words alive. Words like 'stepping out' and 'courting' are so much better than 'hooking up' or 'getting with'. I have always preferred 'paramour' to boyfriend or girlfriend. And 'poppycock' speaks for itself—what a great word. And while the youth might refer to 'pingas' and 'nangs' (although they probably don't anymore but they did at the time I wrote that sentence), I think when it comes to drug language you can't go past words like 'jazz-cabbage' or indeed the very old-fashioned and rather quaint 'pot'. The idea of going up to a dealer and asking for 'three packets of pot, please' really tickles me.

81
Wellness is not a word

I know this word is everywhere now, it's inescapable, but it's as dumb as saying 'healthosity' or 'nutritionative'.

82
The word 'budget' should never be paired with any of the following

- Seafood
- Airline
- Plastic surgery
- Dental work

83
Don't refer to your 'tribe'

Unless you are from an indigenous culture and you genuinely have a tribe. Note, a beard and strident opinions about cold-pressed coffee do not constitute a tribe.

84
Adults do not get to say 'din-dins' or 'nom-noms'

Remember, other people are trying to eat, don't put them off their food.

85
Don't ever mention your 'happy place'

To me, this sounds less like a pleasant, fun state of mind and more like some kind of utopian wank palace you've had built in the basement.

86
Poncewobble is a word, please use it

Every year the *Macquarie Dictionary* accepts a few new words into their dictionary and every year I wait for them to announce that 'poncewobble' is one of those words. Sadly, it hasn't happened yet. I learned about poncewobbling from Jane Faure-Brac, whose brother invented the word sometime during the 1970s. I loved it the first time I heard it.

Poncewobble is a verb and it describes an action that will be recognised by anyone with siblings. Among siblings, there is always one who hoards their treats. Whether it's Easter eggs, contents of showbags or even unopened Christmas presents, the canny hoarder hides their treats and pretends they've eaten them all and that they have nothing left. They may even actively encourage the other siblings to consume all their treats. When they have nothing left, the trickster then brings out all their goodies and takes great delight in eating them slowly in front of the others.

The act of hoarding and hiding with the sole aim of lording it over others later is called poncewobbling. And there's always one poncewobbler (noun) in every family. I'm ashamed to say that in my family it was me. Poncewobbling can have an unfortunate and often unforeseen consequence, and that is when the parent steps in and makes the poncewobbler share their remaining treats with the siblings who have nothing left. Poncewobbling—be careful kids, it's a risky business.

A word about the generation gap

Youth-speak is an area of language that changes faster than any other, therefore it's difficult to make definitive rules about particular words you should or shouldn't use. That's because while youths are great inventers of words and phrases, they also dump those words as fast as they invent them. A basic rule of thumb for anyone over forty who wants to avoid looking out of touch is to listen closely to the vernacular of teenagers and then never use any of the words you just heard. Let the youth enjoy their own language, you have lots of other things, like financial stability and Facebook. (Which, of course, you totally stole from the youth because they were forced to drop it once all the parents and unhappy middle-aged married people discovered it and started using it to track down their high school sweethearts.) Act your age and maintain your dignity by sticking with language from your own era. As embarrassing as it may be to *refer to something as 'bitchin' or 'bodacious', at least you just sound old, as opposed to old **and** try-hard.*

Remember, if you have to ask a youth what the word means, you shouldn't use it. I have listed a few examples here, but this is by no means a definitive list. Also, they were listed at the time of writing, which means that by the time of publication, they may well have disappeared into the vast abyss of discarded youth-speak. The fact that I have heard some of them creeping into use on television suggests they are already out.

Lit. *For the record, I don't know what it means. From the context in which I have heard it used, I gather it is something positive. But that's as much as I can tell you. And again, it's not my business to know. I'm well over forty.*

* *Editor's note: The word 'lit' was recently spotted in a well-known fried chicken chain billboard so it's safe to say 'lit' is now obsolete.*

Dropped. *Pertaining to music, such as a single or an album. If you grew up in a time when big black circles called records were **released** and shiny silver things called CDs **came out**, then you are too old to start telling me that someone's new album is 'dropping'. You should also never refer to 'dropping a beat'. Ever.*

Banging. *You can't erase your middle-agedness simply by listening to young people's radio stations. Sure, you can tune in as a way of staying across current musical trends, but avoid repeating any of the language you hear spoken by the presenters such as 'Wow, this shit is on fire' and 'That song is banging!' Youth presenters, however, always drop their g's so* *it would actually be pronounced bangin', not that it matters because you won't be saying it.*

Nanginator. *This is the name given to the equipment used to 'do a nang'. Or at least it was for a few days in June 2019. Even though the kids will probably have moved on from doing nangs by the time this book comes out, I feel that the word 'nanginator' is so great, it deserves a public airing. If you want to know what a nang is, you'll have to ask a teenager but if you want to purchase a nanginator, I happen to know they are available at most good kitchenware stores. Ask for them by name.*

That said, the youth do not get a free pass on language just because they are young and inventive. There are still some rules and even some words I'd suggest they cut from their lexicon altogether, as you will see in the following section.

⟶

KIDS TODAY

87
Curb your use of the word 'like'

Like is many things; however, it is not an adverb and should not be used as such:

> And so I was, **like**, I cannot believe you are not going to, **like**, eat the dessert I made. And she was, **like**, but it's banoffee pie, which is, **like**, disgusting. It's, **like**, not even pie, it's banana-flavoured mucus on, **like,** a cheesecake base. And I was, **like**, whatever.

As you can tell from the above, I don't particularly **like** banoffee pie.

88
Assume that people know what you mean

Unless you are explaining the solution to a quadratic equation, or you happen to speak in riddles worthy of a cryptic crossword, then it's safe to assume that most people will be able to follow what you're saying. So there's really no need to keep checking in and saying 'know what I mean?' every couple of sentences.

89
Don't use words you don't need, like 'literally'

Most of us don't speak in metaphor and simile, we almost always speak literally, so there is rarely the need to qualify your sentence by adding the word 'literally'. As in 'Oh my god, she ate the whole piece of cake, like, literally the whole piece of cake.'

It would be highly unusual for someone to assume that 'piece of cake' meant something else in this instance so you can do away with the word 'literally'.

However, if you were talking about your dog and how he chewed up one of your board games, then in that instance you might want to qualify your statement with a 'literally': 'We were playing Yahtzee the other day and then Bongo came along and ate the whole box and dice, literally the whole box and dice.'

CONVERSATION

Conversation is the mainstay of any social event, be it a date, a dinner party or a work function. It's something we get to practise all the time, yet very few of us are any good at it and I include myself here. I can talk for an hour and a half on stage **at** *people no problem, but it's very different in social situations.*

I get particularly nervous at parties. I have a real knack of grinding the conversation down into a series of dull questions that the other person has no interest in answering. I've noticed I also ask 'closed questions' a lot of the time, questions that require a short one or two-word answer and never lead to a broader discussion. I know for a fact that I am often 'that person', the one you get trapped talking to and have to invent an excuse to get away from. My saving grace is that I'm aware of my short-comings and when I sense I am dragging someone into one of my conversation death spirals, I will try to help them get away. I will be the one who suggests they move on, saying something like, 'Look, I won't keep you, please go and get yourself a drink', while magnanimously gesturing at the bar with an extended arm, thereby showing them the exit route.

A truly good conversationalist has an uncanny knack of making the person they are talking to feel interesting. It's an amazing skill—usually you don't even realise you're in the presence of a good conversationalist, you just start thinking, Gee I'm telling some good stories today. *Good conversationalists are few and far between, which is a shame because they make social occasions an absolute joy.*

Obviously, as a person completely lacking in conversation skills, I needed to consult some experts to help formulate the following rules. Luckily I know a couple of excellent conversationalists. One is my best friend Glenn. Another is my fellow rule-maker Sophie. I also know a third expert called Dan, a colleague whom I see only occasionally but who never fails to make me feel both interesting and interested. I have watched him have animated and lively discussions with anyone and everyone in a room, including people I would have written off as dull and boring. I reached out to him by email to ask for his tips on how to be a good conversationalist but he didn't reply. I can only assume he was too engrossed in a conversation to answer me.

90
Turn-take

This is the basic rule of conversation. You each take a turn to speak. And you each take a turn to listen. This second bit is quite important. Listening is different to just watching the other person's mouth and waiting for it to stop moving so you can start talking again.

91
The onus is on you to make the conversation interesting

Don't immediately write someone off as boring; most people have something interesting to say and, if you can find a way to ask good questions, you should be able to have an interesting conversation with anyone.

92
Don't interrogate

The vibe you're going for in a conversation is 'gentle inquisition'. No one wants to feel like they're being cross-examined at a murder trial. Subtle coaxing to extract further detail is permissible but don't badger them like a lawyer going after an uncooperative witness.

93
Keep your questions to ten words or less

You're not on Radio National trying to expose a politician for misuse of public funds.

94
Move on rather than resort to air filler phrases

Sometimes, despite the best of intentions, you just run out of stuff to say. Always move on before you start filling the awkward silence with phrases like 'Ahhh, wouldn't be dead for quids' or *'C'est la vie'* or 'Well, here we are'.

95
Don't ask vegetarians why they are vegetarian

It's a question that they are forced to answer every time they sit down for a meal with a new person. It's boring for them and if you're lucky they will shut you down with a non-committal shrug and a vague 'I just prefer not to eat meat.' But if you're unlucky you'll come up against a fundamentalist who will redirect the question right back at you and ask why you're NOT vegetarian. They will then rail at you about cruelty to animals, about how your love of meat is destroying the planet and basically make you feel really guilty about your choices. Either way, there's no satisfactory answer so don't waste anyone's time, including your own, asking the question.

The exception is if you're talking to comedian Dave Hughes, who has quite an interesting answer, which relates to the fact that he used to work in an abattoir and it put him off eating meat for life. It will probably put you off eating meat too, not necessarily for life but at least for a couple of days, so that's good—you can do your bit for the planet, even if it's just for a day or two.

96

Always, however, ask converts why they converted

There is something quite bizarre about grown-up people with solid, tertiary educations converting to one of the traditional book religions. As someone who grew up Catholic and experienced the pointless rituals and praying first-hand, I have never understood how a rational, thinking adult can choose to adopt formalised religion. It's different when you're born into it, you don't know anything else and besides, it's your family, it's your culture.

97

Know when the small talk well is running dry and bail out

'Got any travel plans?' is an acceptable question when you're struggling to sustain a floundering conversation; however, if you then follow it up with 'Oh that's nice . . . so, when do you go away?' the conversation is officially dead in the water. So make an excuse and exeunt. Unless you're planning a burglary of their house, there is nothing to be gained by garnering the exact dates of an acquaintance's holiday.

98

Recounting a TV series to someone in great detail does not constitute good conversation

I do this a lot. Sorry everyone.

99

Have a few emergency 'go-to' questions for when the conversation stalls

Basic conversation starters like:

'Who do you fancy in the Australian Open?'

or

'What's your favourite soup recipe?'

or

'Would you rather be deaf or blind?'

or

'If you could ask Jennifer Aniston one question, what would it be?'

or

'Hand on heart, if you'd had an attic, would you have let Anne Frank hide in there?'

PLANES, TRAINS & AUTOMOBILES

A word about air travel

I admit I seem to have an excessive amount of rules pertaining to planes and airports, but that's because I do a lot of touring and I spend an excessive amount of time on planes and in airports.

I realise there are many people who only fly occasionally and when they do it's almost always for the purpose of a holiday. That puts you in a completely different mindset to those who travel for work purposes. Being in holiday mode means you are far more likely to be in a good mood—you're going somewhere you've been dreaming about, you have no urgent or pressing engagements at the other end—and all that adds up to a person who is far more relaxed and far less likely to get apoplectic about cockheads who stand too close to the baggage carousel. In fact, you might even be one of those cockheads.

FLYING

100
No reclining on short flights

It's already a tight fit on a plane, even for me, and I'm well below average height. For this reason, we must all be a little selfless on planes and consider our fellow travellers, in particular the passenger in the seat directly behind us. If the flight is short, say two hours or less, then sit up. The whole way. Do not recline. After all, if you're *that* tired, you'll be able to fall asleep sitting up. No need to recline with a pillow and a blankie, it's not like you're going to be in the air long enough to enjoy a bit of solid REM sleep. So just sit up and do what all the other more considerate travellers do—doze off for a few minutes and then wake up with a jerk when their head nods forward.

101
Put your kid's seat up and keep it up

Under no circumstances should small children be allowed to recline their seat. This is totally unnecessary and quite possibly the single greatest cause of air-rage on passenger planes today.

102
No bare feet on planes

The only time your feet should be bare is when you are removing one sock in order to place a heavier (or lighter) travel sock on instead. You definitely should not be walking around the cabin in bare feet, and as for going to the toilet barefoot, that is an absolute no-no. Shoes should always be slipped back on for trips to the toilet because I don't know what people are doing in there but I know they're doing it all over the floor.

103
Apparently the person in the middle seat gets both armrests

I confess I did not know this rule; it came courtesy of a well-informed flight attendant so I guess it must be true. It makes sense—there is nothing more punishing than the middle seat, so you deserve some kind of reward and that is both armrests. Apparently.

104
Headphones, headphones, headphones

This is another of those rules that you wouldn't think needed to be stated. Surely, as considerate humans, we have a natural-born instinct to always wear headphones on a plane. Not the case, it turns out. I was on a plane recently where the young woman in front of me was watching a movie on her iPad with no head-phones. After doing a lot of loud 'tsking' and getting no response, I finally leant forward and asked her, very passive-aggressively, if she would like some headphones, and even proffered a set of the complimentary plane headphones at her. She blithely waved me away and chirpily said 'No, thank you.' And I sat back and felt sad. I can't blame her—it's the parents' fault. Headphone usage is something that needs to be taught from an early age. I would suggest that after a child has learned 'Mama' and 'Dada' their next words should be 'headphones, please'.

I am not one of those extremists who advocates for child-free flights; I think that's ridiculous. Rather, children should be welcomed on planes, but the airlines need to take more responsibility and include the headphone rule in the safety briefing. Because it really is a safety issue. I am perfectly happy to play peek-a-boo with your toddler over the back of the chair; I don't even mind if your kid wails a bit. I get it, they're just kids, they get upset about stuff like spilled apple juice and broken crayons. But god help you if you let your kid watch *Peppa Pig* or play some game on an iPad without headphones. I will have you arrested by the Sky Marshall. And if we don't have Sky Marshalls on planes in Australia then I'll tell the flight attendant I overheard you say you have a bomb in your bag.

105
Always nudge a snoring passenger awake

It's perfectly acceptable to 'accidentally' bump a snoring passenger in order to wake them up. In fact, if you are seated next to the snorer, it's your duty to give them a sharp elbow nudge. Snoring passengers have no right of reply; they cannot object to getting nudged. This is another problem that would be better dealt with by the airlines themselves, to prevent any argument or awkwardness between passengers. My suggestion is that a flight attendant should occasionally patrol the aisles with a stick to poke any snoring passengers awake.

106
Do not, under any circumstances, have sex in the toilet

What is wrong with people? If anyone ever boasts to me about how they've joined the 'Mile High Club', my only thought is, *Ewwwww, you had sex in a tiny cramped toilet that four hundred-odd people have been poohing and weeing in. You disgust me.*

* *Author's note: This book was originally written and published in 2019 when Wuhan was just another city rather than a punchline for every Covid joke ever made. And even before the pandemic was raging all around us, many suggested that these flying rules should be compulsory pre-flight information. As this updated edition goes to print, most airlines are still operating largely restricted services but hopefully, one day, we will get back in the air. When that happens, I hope that the following two rules will be passed into law. Or at least be included on the seat-back pocket safety card.*

107
Maximum three sniffs, then get a tissue

This is a universal rule but nowhere is it more important than on a plane, where those around you are trapped in their seats and unable to move away from your incessant and unrelenting sniffing.

108
Accept the lozenge

I've always been nervy about coughers on planes, well before Covid-19 struck. Coughing on planes really puts me on edge. After all, it's a limited amount of air we're sharing up there. And my assumption was that those coughed-up germs would eventually end up blowing directly onto my face courtesy of that little outlet above my head. The longer the coughing went on, the more panicky I would become. By the time the pilot landed that flying bacteria tube, I'd be convinced everyone on board was infected with SARS or swine flu or even good old-fashioned Ebola. Ohhh remember those viruses? The ones we *did* manage to contain? Seems like a lifetime ago that we were worried about something as silly as bleeding from our eyeballs. Point is, I always made a mental note of the cougher's seat number in case an outbreak occurred and I needed to inform the authorities. I've watched enough biohazard movies to know the importance of being able to track down Patient Zero.

This is why lozenges are essential. Not only because I don't want to be the cougher on the plane but also so that I am able to offer a lozenge to a fellow coughing passenger. 'Lozenge, sir?' is the politest way of saying, 'For the love of god, you're going to kill us all, stop coughing!' So if you are ever offered a lozenge, please take it and suck it and let's save some lives.

109
Keep walking when you hit the moving footway

Moving footways are designed to make your journey through the airport a little faster, to speed you along as you walk. However, most people use them to see what life would be like if they lost the use of their legs. The minute they hit that moving rubber walkway, they stop dead, no longer able to put one leg in front of the other.

110
No bunching

Ordinarily, Australians are very good about personal space and not standing too close to one another but, for some reason, in airports all bets are off. Something about the proximity to planes brings out people's inner urge to bunch right up behind you.

Bunching starts as soon as you arrive with people 'accident-ally' nudging their luggage into the backs of your legs as they stand too close behind you in the check-in queue. And the bad news is that's just the beginning—the bunching doesn't stop until you're actually in a cab leaving the airport at the other end of your journey.

111
Only people in the aisle seats may stand up before the door is opened

When the plane lands and the seatbelt sign goes off, usually what happens is everyone leaps up and tries to move out into the aisle, however, you must only do that if you are seated *on* the aisle. Everyone else needs to wait patiently in their seats. You can stand up, if you're short like me and won't hit your head, but you can't move out into the aisle. You physically can't. It's Archimedes' displacement principle—you can't just keep pouring more bodies into the aisle without it overflowing. And there's nowhere for it to overflow to until they open the door at the front of the plane.

So stop thinking you can defy science and accept that there is only one way to get off a plane and that is single file, in an orderly fashion, row by row, once the door is actually opened. If you are seated in the last row of the plane, you're getting off last, there's nothing you can do about it, that's just how it works.

112
Stand back from the baggage carousel

The baggage carousel is where the mother of all bunching occurs. It's like all that other bunching throughout the trip was a mere rehearsal for the main event at the baggage carousel. People stand three and four rows deep around the carousel, pushing right up to the edge of it, making it difficult for anyone not in the front row to see their bag, let alone access it. If everyone would stand back a bit, then we would all be able to see and we would all be able to get in and out to retrieve our bags. And a note to parents, collecting the bags should not be viewed as a fun holiday activity for the whole family: move the kids back. Appoint one designated bag collector and everyone else can stay out of the fray and act as spotters.

My dream is that airports will one day paint a thick yellow demarcation line around the carousel perimeter that creates a one-metre 'no standing zone' around the whole carousel. And it will be against the law to be caught standing inside that yellow line UNLESS you are physically removing your bag from the carousel.

SPECIAL SEALED SECTION
SCOOCHING

If you don't fly much, you can skip this next part; you have already suffered enough reading through my many rules about planes and airports. This section is specifically written for people who fly all the time and yet still don't understand how to move through the security check efficiently. The secret is scooching.

→

113
Scooch your bags right to the end
of the security conveyer belt

If I was shopping for a husband, I would go to the airport and watch people move through security. Anyone who gets it right is marriage material.

Heading into the security check, things aren't too bad, sometimes there's a bit of mild bunching but overall it's a fairly orderly procedure. Passengers use the entire length of the conveyor belt and shuffle or 'scooch' their stuff towards the X-ray machine.

Airside, however, everything grinds to a halt as passengers crowd the exit mouth of the X-ray machine, desperate to grab their items and start repacking their bags as soon as things emerge.

The flaw in the system is that people pass through the metal detector faster than bags pass through the X-ray. Add to that the complication that most people are waiting on more than one item. There's your bag, plus the laptop you removed from your bag, and there might be an aerosol and/or a belt etc. in another tray. If you're a novice traveller who doesn't know the rules for domestic flights, you might also have dumped all your liquids and toiletries into yet another tray. (Note to the novice; you only have to do that on international flights. Oh and there's no need to urgently suck down your 500 ml of Gatorade or iced tea or vitamin water either, you can take it with you. Kudos to the security staff who stand idly by and let those chumps chug half a litre of fluid instead of letting them know they're allowed to take it through; it certainly does make entertaining viewing for everyone else in the queue.)

The solution to the multiple bags and resulting pile-up of people hovering around the exit mouth of the X-ray, is scooching. You pass through the metal detector, take a brief turn at the exit mouth and scooch. No grabbing and repacking or sorting, just vigorously scooch any items that appear, be they yours or someone else's, scooch those mothers right down to the end of the conveyor belt. *Then* you can move yourself along the conveyor belt, out of the hot zone, and do all your repacking and re-belting business *down at the far end*. A little less grabbing and a bit more scooching would really help to keep things moving and prevent bunching.

ON THE ROAD

I don't suffer from road rage. That said, there's a good chance I incite a lot of it with my slow nanna-style driving. I sit very close to the steering wheel and I rarely do the speed limit —40 seems ample in a built-up area, and as for doing 110 on a freeway? Christ, I don't know if I could take the g-forces, I'm not Iceman in Top Gun.

The only time I become enraged on the road is when I allow a fellow motorist to cross into my lane or pull out into the flow of traffic and that person fails to raise a hand and tip me a thank-you wave. In that instance it takes all my self-control not to 'go the chase'. I am overcome with the urge to follow them home and sit outside their house with my hand stuck on the horn until they come out and acknowledge my magnanimous gesture. Which is why my first rule of the road is:

114
Courtesy waves are mandatory

When someone lets you in to traffic, acknowledge the act with a wave. Always. No exceptions. Courtesy breeds courtesy and thank-you waves spread goodwill on the roads.

115
Courtesy waves from pedestrians are strongly encouraged

Yes, the law says that the driver must stop to allow you to cross at a pedestrian crossing, but that doesn't mean you shouldn't still give them a tip of the hat for doing so. I love a pedestrian who offers a smile and a nod to the driver as they cross, it's a real mood-lifter.

116
Be ready at the red light

Being first at the red light is a high-pressure position. And as such you must not do anything but stare at that red light and wait for it to change. No checking your makeup or your phone, don't start searching for a podcast or glancing at texts, just watch the red light. You need to be like a coiled spring, at the ready (riding the clutch if need be, keeping the car humming at friction point), so that the minute the light changes to green you can take off and allow as many cars as possible to get through that intersection. That's courteous driving.

117
Vacate the car space if you can see someone is waiting

Don't be that person who pops their stuff in the boot, jumps in the driver's seat, then sits there and doesn't leave despite the fact that someone else has pulled up alongside, put their indicator on and is now holding up the traffic waiting for you to move on. If you can see a person waiting for the parking space, get out of there, don't start making calls or sending texts, you're not the Lincoln Lawyer, the car isn't your office, just drive off and relinquish the parking space.

118
It's a car not a pencil case

No need to put stickers all over it. No one cares what radio station you listen to or that you shoot and vote, or that you have two stick figure children, a stick figure dog and a stick figure wife who likes surfing. No one cares that you shut the gate or lock the gate or whatever the latest thing is with gates and fracking. Most people *don't* support fracking so really you should only need a sticker if you want to tell people you're really into it, maybe a sticker that says *Fracking! It's a gas gas gas!* or *My water is on fire! I heart fracking.*

119
Men don't look good driving convertible cars

There is simply no age where it looks right for a man to be driving a convertible car. If you're late teens/early twenties, you look like a spoilt child whose parents have bought you a convertible. If you're early thirties, you look like an investment banker who's bought the car as a personality proxy. If you're in your forties, you look like you're having a midlife crisis, and if you're any older than that you look like you've been told you have six months to live so you've chucked it all in and bought a convertible. Convertibles look better on women.

120
Reverse parking is not a spectator sport

Reverse parking is always a slightly tricky manoeuvre, but doing it in front of an audience—such as when you're parking outside a crowded cafe—increases the level of difficulty tenfold. Do the parker a courtesy and avert your eyes while they park. Do not, under any circumstances, settle into position, kick back and watch the 'show'. It only makes the task harder and far less likely to happen in one neat attempt.

121
The horn is not a toy, use it sparingly

People who honk out of rage and frustration should be fined and their horn should be removed from their vehicle. I'm talking about those people who don't understand that holding your hand flat on the horn and honking it continually does not move the traffic forward. The red light can't hear you. And that traffic accident up ahead won't miraculously clear because you long-honked it.

The horn should only be used to deliver friendly reminders or alerts to fellow motorists. It's a way to say, 'Hey buddy, light's gone green!' or 'Yoohoo! I think you'll find traffic is on the move again.' Or 'Mate! Mate! Mate! Stop reversing, I'm right here behind you!' And the way you communicate those things is with a light touch. No pressing hard on the horn and making it wail like a bagpipe, that's not helping.

I would like to see horn-use included on the driving test. Before being awarded a licence, the learner driver should be required to demonstrate the various types of friendly honk such as: an amiable 'toot toot', a light 'parp' and, my favourite, a gentle 'mip mip'. Any flat-handed honking would be an immediate fail.

PUBLIC TRANSPORT

122
Don't sit next to someone unless there is no alternative

Basically this means that if you get on a bus or a tram and there is a completely empty seat available, you are obligated to take that seat, even if you have to walk a bit further to get to it. Don't be a space invader and sit down to rub thighs with a stranger when there are still 'full empties' available.

123
Headphones, headphones, headphones

This rule has already appeared in the plane travel section; however, it is also an important rule on every other form of public transport.

124
Don't wait to be asked to move your bag off the seat

I don't mind people putting their bags on the seat next to them, sometimes it's just easier than putting them on the floor. But if the bus or tram starts to fill up, don't take the piss, don't wait to be asked, just take your bags off the seat.

125
Stand up for old people

I love seeing an old person using public transport. Not only does it mean they are keeping active and getting out and about but, better still, it means they are not behind the wheel of a car driving the wrong way around a roundabout or accelerating into cafes by accident. Let's encourage even more of them to get off the roads and onto public transport by making sure it's always an easy and pleasant journey—and the way to do that is by standing up and offering them a seat.

126
No talking at all in the quiet carriage

The rule is no talking. Not, no talking on your mobile phone—no talking, *at all*. There is usually only one quiet carriage but there are many non-quiet ones where you suited gentlemen can conduct your loud boring work conversations about KPIs and target demographics that no one else is interested in!

127
Don't lean your whole body against
the pole in the train vestibule

It makes it impossible for other standing passengers to hold onto the pole without groping you in unseemly places.

FOOD

GENERAL FOOD RULES

128
Avocado is a salad item

It doesn't belong in pasta. And it really doesn't belong in smoothies, what a waste of money. For an extra five bucks all you're doing is adding a totally tasteless, pale green hue to your beverage and making it even more difficult to suck through a straw.

129
No tomato in guacamole

My book, my rules. And besides, tomato makes your guacamole watery and weird tasting.

130
Dark chocolate is not a treat

We all know this to be true. But for some reason health and 'wellness' types refuse to admit it. They talk up dark chocolate like it's some kind of delicious sinful pleasure, always going on about how you only need 'one square' as an after-dinner treat. Of course you only need one square, the stuff is bitter and unpleasant. Personally, I don't even want one square. Milk chocolate, however, I can poke that in my pie-hole row after delicious row!

131
Calling it 'cacao' doesn't make it healthier than cocoa

You just moved a few letters around. Stop kidding yourself.

132
The only thing more disappointing
than dark chocolate is carob

Except for the fact that they are both brown, carob is nothing like chocolate. As for being a good chocolate substitute, this is true only in the same way that sand is a good substitute for sugar. Giving carob to your children and telling them it's 'yummy chocky' is tantamount to child abuse.

133
Don't get fancy with lettuce

Iceberg lettuce is crisp, it's crunchy, it's got enough structural integrity to hold up to a thick dressing and it's a terrific salad workhorse. You can throw in a few other leaves for decoration but if you're looking for a solid, crowd-pleasing base, go with iceberg.

134
A poke bowl is not a dumping ground
for the contents of your fridge

Some people mistakenly think poke bowl means 'poke whatever you can find into a bowl'. Yes, the poke bowl is a convenient and easy way to make a meal, but you still need to pick some kind of theme for your melange of ingredients. Whether it's Asian, Italian, traditional Hawaiian, whatever, you must be consistent with your flavours. An example of something that is definitely not a poke bowl is this random set of ingredients: rice, spinach, tomato, three-bean mix and satay-flavoured tofu.

One of my fellow rule-makers witnessed that combination being 'poked' together in a bowl by a colleague in the office kitchen. She was so horrified, she texted me to report it. She was (rightly) appalled by the disgusting mash-up of flavours. I, too, was aghast; however, I was also intrigued by the mention of three-bean mix? I didn't even know you could still get that stuff? I thought it was like tinned asparagus, just a distant and unpleasant-smelling memory from the 1970s.

135
You can't juice a guava

Don't believe the label that says 'guava juice'. There's nothing at all juicy about guavas. What you're really getting is a glass of thick, fibrous pink paste. Blergh.

136
Don't spend money on water

Doesn't matter how 'artisanal' it is, or how pretty the shape or colour of the bottle, it's still just water and you can get exactly the same thing out of the tap.

137
Keep your new food regime to yourself

Whether you've given up sugar or carbs or maybe you're fasting two days a week on the ol' 5-2, perhaps you're eating like a caveman or limiting your FODMAPs or your bibimbaps; whatever your new regime is, don't go on about it. For while I have nothing but respect for people who can be strict about their food intake, it's really boring when that's all they talk about.

I don't want to hear about your cheat days or your eight cups of green tea or your pale, straw-coloured urine or your 'delicious

one square of dark chocolate' and I really don't want to be out
to dinner with you when you grill the waitress about the ingredients and preparation method of every single dish on the menu.

138
Taste your meal before you salt it

This is a rule for old people who habitually reach for the salt
and shake astonishing amounts of the stuff all over their food
before they've even tasted it. Honestly, I could serve sea-water
soup to my parents and they would still go at it with the salt.
And I'm not saying you can't add salt, I'm saying you should do
whoever has cooked the meal the courtesy of tasting it first, just
one mouthful to consider the flavours and the subtle seasonings,
then tip your salt all over it.

EATING

139
Eat like someone is watching

I don't care how you dance but you should always eat like someone is watching. People who live alone need be particularly vigilant about this. When you eat on your own, there's no one to keep you in check and it's easy to get lazy. There's no one to look appalled when you use your fork like a shovel and hurl food into your mouth like coal into a locomotive steam engine. No one to shake their head gently and say, 'too much, too much' when you try to poke a whole piece of sushi or roast potato into your mouth at once. Always eat 'with awareness' to avoid developing bad habits that may shock others next time you are eating in company.

140
Don't overload your fork

If you can't get your forkful of food straight from the plate to your mouth without having to turn or rotate the fork in order to push everything into your mouth, then there's too much on it. Put your fork down, take a little bit off and try again. There should be no complex manoeuvring required, you're eating, not reverse parking food into your mouth.

141
Whatever goes in your mouth stays in your mouth

This rule tends to be abandoned when people eat spaghetti. We've all witnessed the human sausage mincer sitting opposite, with a long trail of spaghetti hanging out of their mouth that they bite off and let fall back into the bowl. Twirl it on your fork, people, twirl it on your fork, get all your strands secure and then put it in your mouth. Or order penne. Especially if you're on a date; never order spaghetti, always request penne.

142
Don't order bucatini if you're hungry

Bucatini is that thick spaghetti pasta with a hole running down the centre of it. It's an incredibly difficult pasta to manage because you can't suck it into your mouth like you can spaghetti and it doesn't wrap easily around your fork as it's so thick. Plus the hole in the middle means you can't get any purchase. You can suck all you like but you're just pulling in air, it's like a pasta straw. All this makes for a very time-consuming meal and I don't recommend it, especially if you're hungry.

143
No 'smack-smacking'

Smack-smacking is a term that describes chewing with your mouth open. It pertains to the disgusting masticatory sound of food and saliva smacking together and then being amplified by the chewer's flapping gums. All you hear is 'Smack smack smack smack smack' echoing out of their gaping cake-hole.

This is another one of those rules that you wouldn't think needed to be written down. Just as Labradors are born knowing how to retrieve, surely humans should be born knowing that chewing with your mouth open is dizz-gusting.

144
No chipmunking

Chipmunking is the act of pushing food into the side of your mouth so you can talk with your mouth full. So-called because you look like a fat-faced little chipmunk when you do it—only a lot less adorable. I confess I break this rule a lot and need constant reprimanding. It must be genetic, because every member of my family is a chronic chipmunker. We love to eat and we love to talk and sometimes we find it hard to decide which of those things to prioritise.

145
Chew your food, don't inhale it

I have a tendency to get overexcited about food, which means I often eat too quickly. It's important to remember no one is coming to take your food. And it's not a race, there are no prizes for eating fast—and, if there are, you should leave that establishment immediately. Eating contests are for idiots.

146
Sit down to eat

You can't enjoy your food while you're wandering around. Sit down. Eat properly. In parts of Japan they fine you for walking and eating, and if I have my way we'll soon introduce that law in Australia too.

147
'All you can eat' is not an order

It's not compulsory to eat as much as you can just because you're at an all-you-can-eat buffet. You are allowed to go to the buffet and simply eat what my mother would call 'an elegant sufficiency'. To be clear, I'm not exactly sure what that is but, if I had to guess, I'd say it means 'Don't eat so much that you fall into a food coma.'

148
'One plate only' is not a challenge

Some places offer an all-you-can-eat dining experience with the added restriction of one plate only. For Australians, this seems to encourage them to eat more than ever. They go at that buffet determined to make sure they don't get ripped off. This is why you see people carefully constructing Jenga-style towers of food, building their meal up in layers so as to fit as much as possible on their one plate. It's no longer about what they would like to eat, or how hungry they are, it's about getting their money's worth. But to what end? Yes, you're 'screwing' the system, but you're also screwing your dining experience. Who can possibly enjoy a plate of beef stroganoff, flattened out by a chicken schnitzel topped with a layer of potato wedges and then stacked high with fourteen 'fresh' king prawns and three dodgy-looking oysters nestled on the top. You may as well go and eat straight from the dumpster out the back.

DINING OUT

149
Lift your chair

Whether you're pulling it out to sit down or placing it back under the table when you leave, lift your chair. Don't drag it across the floor and make that hideous honking scraping sound: lift it. If you don't have the strength to lift your chair, perhaps you'd be better served at the gym than the cafe.

150
Be polite to waitstaff

There is nothing more odious and embarrassing than being with someone who speaks rudely to waiters. Also, you're playing with fire; think about it, they have access to your food, you don't know what they're going to do to it in the kitchen. Be nice.

151
Don't steal the pepper grinder

Obviously people do this and that's why cafes adopted the practice of having a single pepper grinder the size of a small child that the waiter brings to the table briefly and then swiftly removes. Please stop nicking the pepper grinders so we can all pepper our own food like grown-ups.

152
The waiter is not Judge Judy

So don't call them over and say 'Settle an argument for us, would you ...'

153
Don't expect the chef to accommodate your food fad

Most restaurants post their menu online, so if you have a highly restrictive diet (by choice rather than because you have allergies) then check the menu first and, if it doesn't suit your new regime, don't go to that restaurant. Or maybe take a brief respite from your diet and enjoy a one-off meal with everything in it. Whatever you do, just don't ask the chef to change their signature dish to suit your dietary whims. That's rude. And so presumptuous. They run a restaurant, you came to them, they're not your personal chef.

154
Respect the non-drinker at the table

Make a mental note if someone is not drinking and don't make them pay for alcohol. It's bad enough they have to stay sober and observe the rest of the table getting loose and starting to talk too loudly and make lamo 'jokes' with the waitstaff. Don't make them pay for the privilege as well. Being the only sober person at a table of drinkers is punishment enough.

155
Don't punish the vegetarian

If there is a vegetarian at a dinner where all the dishes are being shared, then either order plenty of vegetarian dishes for everyone to enjoy or lay off that one vegetarian dish at the table. It's galling for vegetarians to watch everyone hoeing into the only dish they can eat—and even more annoying when all the meat-eaters start going on about how delicious that one vegetarian dish is.

CAFES AND RESTAURANTS

156
Waiters, write it down

No one will think any less of you. Trust me when I say that nobody is impressed by the fact that you (apparently) are able to remember everything without writing it down. On the contrary, you're making everyone at the table feel tense. We're all sitting there thinking, *I bet he gets **my** order wrong.*

157
Don't hand out numbers on sticks

Nothing tempers your dining experience faster than finding out you have to order at the counter and then walk around the cafe wielding a number on a stick while you look for a table.

Ordering at the counter is particularly tricky for the single diner. When there are two people, one can hold the table while the other goes to order. But as the lonely lady diner, it's hard to claim a table until you've actually ordered. You have to either prematurely disrobe in order to leave an item of clothing draped across a chair, or remove something not particularly valuable from your bag and deposit that on the table. Something like a book or a pair of spectacles (but it can't be a Kindle or sunglasses because someone might steal those things). I don't always carry a bag so I've been left in the unfortunate position of trying to stake a claim on a table by leaving the contents of my pocket on it—a lip gloss, a pen and a dirty tissue. If you don't do this and the cafe is crowded, then you run the risk of having nowhere to sit and eat the food you've just ordered and paid for.

Brisbane cafes are notorious for the order at the counter feature. Time to step it up, Brisbane; you're an international city.

158
Jokes on cafe chalkboards do not bring in clientele

It's the promise of good coffee that draws people into a cafe, not a pithy gag on a chalkboard, like this one I saw recently: *My friend told me I was delusional, I nearly fell off my unicorn!* Hmm, perhaps if they were a better friend, they'd have told you not to write those words on a chalkboard outside your cafe. The problem is, these things are mildly amusing the first time you read them but you need to commit to a new one every day, otherwise you just annoy people. I have walked past this particular gem half a dozen times in the last week—*Jesus was a Carpenter but he didn't sing on any of the albums*—and it's starting to feel like I'm at a party standing with a drunk person who keeps telling me the same unfunny story again and again. Why not just write something that will stand the test of time and be appreciated every day like, *Come on in, we don't charge four dollars for a latte!*

159
No communal dishes of sea salt

Sure, that miniature bowl containing a mound of salt (that everyone is dipping their grubby fingers into) *looks* aesthetically pleasing, but in reality it is a potpourri of pathogens. I know specialty salt is all the rage now, with many varieties like truffle salt and lemon myrtle salt, but I think we can all agree to live without bacteria salt. Bring back the saltshaker.

160
Don't serve coffee in abnormal drinking vessels

Coffee should be served in cups or Duralex-style glasses only. No mugs. And definitely no tall, glass mug-things. I'm referring to those highly impractical latte glasses some cafes use in a bid to be fancy. Sometimes they're straight-sided, other times they have sloping sides so you feel like you're drinking coffee from a small vase or glass urn. What they all have in common is the small, useless, circular handle positioned in the lower part of the glass.

Apart from being stupid-looking, these tall glass mug-things have a very basic design flaw, in that the position of the handle means the fulcrum is too low, which makes for a difficult, unbalanced and unenjoyable drinking experience. On top of that, they don't stack, which makes them a completely impractical item in a cafe with limited space. They do seem to be more common in 'order at the counter' establishments so I guess I'm looking at you again, Brisbane.

161
Only roadside diners should serve jam in little plastic packets

If you purport to be a cafe and you have toast and jam on the menu (that you're no doubt charging out at five or six bucks a pop), take thirty seconds to show your customers you care by decanting some quality jam from a jar into a small dish. Those nasty little plastic packets on the plate make your establishment look cheap. Also, they're too small; it's not nearly enough jam for two pieces of toast. Or butter for that matter. Two pats of butter per piece, please.

162

Don't try to guess my income, just bring tapwater

Being asked 'Do you want still or sparkling water?' as soon as you sit down at a restaurant feels like a rather unsubtle way of asking whether the customer is cashed up or a cheapskate. Restaurants should assume that everyone wants water and simply bring tap water to the table on arrival.

If the customer is appalled by the idea of drinking water from a tap, they will no doubt make it known and request some overpriced bottled still water. Same goes for sparkling water. If someone wants it, they'll ask for it. No one has ever sat in a restaurant thinking, *Hmm, they haven't mentioned sparkling water . . . they probably don't have it, best not to make a fool of myself by asking for it.*

163

If the avocado is hard as a rock, don't serve it

And don't even think about charging five bucks extra for it as a side order.

164

Don't serve food on planks, tiles, slabs of granite or any other building materials

Bowls and plates are more than adequate. If in doubt as to whether a vessel is suitable for food service, check that there is some kind of lip or edge to it—you need enough to keep your food from constantly falling off onto the table and to stop any food from shooting across at the diner opposite you should your knife or fork slip.

165
Leave room between tables for a standard-sized caboose

It's never enjoyable when cafes put tables too close together. It's humiliating to have to slide your bum across the next table's eating surface whenever you squeeze yourself in or out.

166
Tip jar gags reduce your chances of getting a tip

It's best to play it safe and simply write *TIPS* on the tip jar. Not *Staff Retirement Fund, Give Generously—Winky face* or *Tip it, Tip it Good!* or *If you fear change, leave it with us!* And under no circumstances should you sex shame your patrons at the counter: *Generous tippers make generous lovers.* Eww.

167
Enforce the 'Please wait to be seated' sign

I'm a big fan of cafes and restaurants that like to control the flow of customers into their establishment. I love an orderly system and I love it when there's no ambiguity as to what the system is, which is why I like it when I see a *Please wait to be seated* sign. However, if you are going to make such a bold claim about having a system, then someone must be on hand to implement that system. You need a designated greeter. Without a greeter keeping tabs on arrivals and doing the job of greeting and seating, what happens is the obedient people like myself stand at the entrance for ages, like dolts, while flagrant rule-breakers barge past and claim all the tables. You can't rely on your regular waitstaff to fill the greet and seat role because the minute they get busy they will suddenly develop 'waiter vision impairment syndrome', which is when they pretend they can't see you or anyone else in the queue of well-behaved patrons standing patiently at the door.

168
Don't make me curate my own lunch

At lunchtime, everyone is in a hurry. No one has the time to stand at the counter and choose a base and then a protein and then a 'crunch' plus one optional extra topping for free and any further toppings for a dollar each (except for avocado, that's two dollars) plus a dressing. You lost me at step two of your five-step process, I've just walked next door to order the number 12 sandwich.

169
Put the parmesan cheese down and walk away

Leave it at the table. Don't dole it out in polite, but insufficient quantities or make me feel like a cheese-pig by calling you back three times to get some more. Just leave it at the table. Let me be in charge of the cheese.

SPECIAL SEALED SECTION
FRUIT

You might think this is going to be a section where I upbraid people for not categorising their fruits and vegetables correctly. However, I actually find that whole fruit vs vegetable thing rather tedious. Certain people delight in shouting you down for calling a tomato a vegetable. 'It's a fruit! The tomato is a fruit! It has seeds! It's a fruit!' These are the same people who can't wait to tell you that the peanut is a legume and that the potato is a deadly nightshade. Yawn. Who cares? As far as I'm concerned there are far more important rules about fruit.

$\longrightarrow$

170
Fruit is not dessert

This is actually my sister's rule. She is forever disappointed when someone offers fruit for dessert. She maintains that fruit can only be categorised as dessert if it is sprinkled with sugar and served with ice cream. Another friend of mine goes further and insists fruit is only dessert if it is smothered in custard. And then there's my mother who thinks that a single, plain, unadorned piece of fruit is the *only* way to finish a meal. I'm somewhere in between these two camps when it comes to fruit. For me, it all comes down to selection and preparation.

171
No filler fruits in fruit salad

Fruit salad can be absolutely delicious; however, all too often it is spoiled by the inclusion of what I call 'filler fruits'. Things like oranges and apples and, god forbid, banana. These are clearly stand-alone fruits, they are supposed to be consumed as a single piece; they're not for cutting up and throwing into the salad melange. Especially banana. The strong flavour of a banana permeates the whole salad and makes everything taste of banana; it also has an unpleasant mucilaginous quality that coats all the other fruits with brownish slime. Apple is also problematic because it goes brown and looks unpalatable within half an hour. And too many people cut up bits of orange without properly removing the pith, so you have to suffer all that white, leathery stuff on every piece. The easiest solution is to leave these fruits out of the fruit salad.

172
The fruit salad in the display cabinet is a mirage

We've all stood at the shop counter and been fooled by the delicious-looking tray of fruit salad. There's a whole healthy mountain of fruity goodness piled high (apparently) with strawberries and watermelon and passionfruit and all the top shelf fruits that you actually enjoy eating, like blueberries and sometimes even mango. Yet when the man behind the counter reaches in with his big silver spoon and shovels out your serve, somehow you don't get any of that top layer, you end up with what lies beneath—those sad, pastel chunks of unripe rockmelon and honeydew melon, and occasionally a few anaemic cubes of fibrous, tasteless pineapple—and if it's a really shitty place, no doubt there'll also be a fair share of those filler fruits I mentioned in the previous rule.

If you're lucky you might get one or two slivers of strawberry but that's it. Turns out those 'whole' strawberries on the top are a complete trompe l'oeil, placed there to lure you in. The rest of the strawberries in the salad (all four of them) have been carefully shaved into about half a dozen wafer-thin slices and sprinkled parsimoniously throughout.

173
There is a right way to cut up an orange

Oranges were the original PowerBars of sport. Each week at netball games across the land, one player's mother would be tasked with bringing out a Tupperware box of cut-up oranges and handing them round to the hot sweaty kids. I don't know who invented that tradition, I'm guessing some smart farmer from orange-growing country. At our netball games, we'd suck on an orange quarter while the coach reminded us to use everyone on the team not just Lauren Fraser. (Lauren Fraser was easily the best player we had and she'd also get really red in the face and yell at you if you didn't pass her the ball. People always think it must be hard for kids who aren't good at sport; I think it must be harder for kids who *are* good at it—they're the ones who would be winning every week if only they weren't on teams full of useless kids who constantly let them down. Sorry, Lauren.)

Orange duty was rotated around the mothers, so my own mum only had to do it once every eight weeks. And that was a shame, because she was the only one who knew the right way to cut up an orange and I think that's because she invented it. I implored her week after week to tell the other mothers how to do it but she was either too smart to do something as dumb as tell another woman how to cut up fruit or she just didn't care. Maybe a bit of both. My mum wasn't big on watching six hopeless idiots and one Lauren run around a netball court on a cold winter's day. My dad would stand on the sidelines and get involved, but my mum would sit in the car with the heater on, occasionally cracking the window to call out, 'I'm watching! I can see you from here!'

So for all you netball mums and dads and anyone else who wants to know the right way to cut up an orange, I have included a diagram of my mother's simple technique. It guarantees six perfect segments of orange with not a scrap of white pith on any piece. Because nobody likes the white bit.

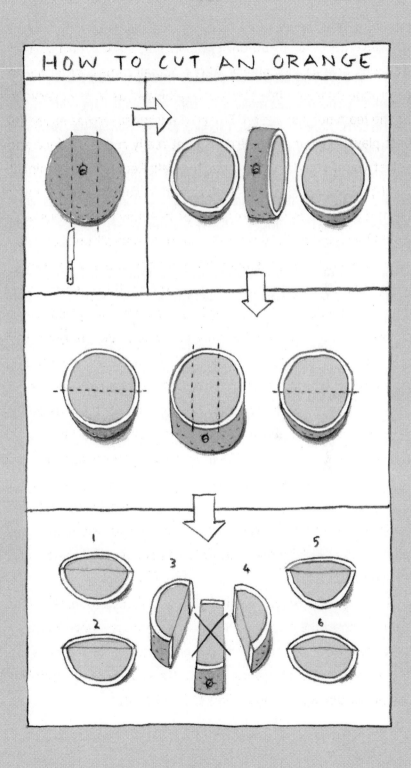

174
Everything on a fruit platter needs to be edible

Essentially this means: make an effort with your fruit platter. Cut the rind off the watermelon, the skin off the pineapple (*properly*, don't leave any of those hard, spiky brown eyes in it) and peel the kiwi fruit; you might even want to hull your strawberries before putting them on a platter. What you don't want is for your guests to have to go looking for the green waste bin every time they finish a bit of fruit.

Grapes are welcome on the platter, despite the inevitable 'stalk waste'. Make sure they have been snipped into smaller, more manageable, mini-bunches of five to seven grapes. No one should be wandering around your party like a Roman emperor at an orgy, head tilted back, lowering an entire bunch of grapes into their gaping maw.

And cherries are the exception to the rule. Cherries are such a treat, everyone will love you for including them on the platter. I'll happily shove a handful of cherry pips in my pocket if I can't find a bin or a little side dish to put them in, cherries are so great!

RELATIONSHIPS & DATING

A word about mixed messages

A friend of mine set me up with a man once. The man was the brother of my friend's friend which is a good degree of separation for matchmaking. You never want it to be too close to home in case it goes wrong. I know some people hate the idea of a set-up but I'm all for it, after all, who knows you better than your friends and family? Surely being set up by a friend makes more sense than online dating or going out to public places and sitting in the corner looking hopeful. And at the time this set-up occurred, I'd been single for so long I was even contemplating asking my mum if any of her friends had sons whose marriages were on the rocks and looked likely to be coming back on the market.

According to my friend, this man—let's call him George (even though his name was Ben)—was just my type. And as it turned out, my friend was right. 'George' was really nice—he was smart and funny and attractive. We went out, had a couple of drinks, the conversation was interesting and easy and I was thinking, Well, this is just perfect, what a great couple we make and we already have mutual friends! I can't wait for us all to get together and have dinner and laugh about why this never happened sooner! Why are people so weird about being set up? George and I are perfect for each other. I wonder when we'll get married . . .

There was only one tiny thing wrong with George and that was that he didn't feel the same way about me. I can't imagine why not. I mean I'm so easygoing, it's not like I have 488 rules about everything from fruit to flatulating. I guess I just wasn't his cup of tea. Unfortunately, George was also very polite, so I had no clue that I wasn't his cup of tea.

*After our hugely successful (I thought) first date, I texted him and suggested another date; he said he was busy but maybe another time, so I texted again. And again. And by the third 'I'm a bit busy at the moment', the penny finally dropped and it dawned on me that he wasn't interested. Actually, maybe it didn't. Now that I think about it, I'm pretty sure my friend had to tell me George wasn't interested. Poor George must have called his sister and said, 'Hey, can you tell **your** friend to tell **his** friend to back off, she keeps texting me and I'm clearly not interested!' The message was passed along and by the time it got to me, I think it had been diluted a bit so as not to totally crush my feelings. I imagine it started out as, 'Jesus, tell that idiot to take a hint, I don't want to go on another date!' to 'Um . . . he's very busy at work and doesn't have time for a relationship right now' to 'I'm pretty sure he just broke up with someone* and he's not in the right headspace at the moment.' In the end, they all mean the same thing: 'He's not interested.' And sure, my pride was a little hurt, but sometimes a reality check can be useful—it's not a bad thing to realise that not everyone thinks you're the bee's knees.

Over a year later, I got a text from George telling me that he'd just seen me on some comedy gala on TV and had really enjoyed my work. He was very complimentary and he signed off the text with an 'x'. I showed it to my friend who immediately said, you should text him, maybe he's in the right headspace now. And so, like an idiot I did. I texted and suggested we go for a drink and guess what? George said yes! We set a date for the following week. The night before our date, George texted to say something had come up and asked if we could reschedule. I said sure and we set another date. Then a few days later he texted to ask if we could raincheck again to the following week. This time I called him because I felt emboldened and like I wanted to be insulted in person rather than just via text. 'Hello, George,' I said (even though his name was Ben). 'It's Kitty here. Listen, do you want to just cancel and forget this whole thing?'

If I'm being completely honest, I thought he would apologise profusely and say, 'No, no, no, I really want to do this, I'm just having trouble finding a free night', but he didn't. He sounded extremely relieved and said, 'Yes! I'm sorry, do you mind? I don't know why I said yes in the first place.' Now I don't mind if someone doesn't want to go out with me but, if you're **not** interested then my advice would be don't send me complimentary texts out of the blue and definitely don't sign those texts with an 'x'. In fact, the next time you see me on the telly and think I'm funny, maybe just think it, don't text it. I guess if there was a rule here, it would be, don't send x's to someone you have no interest in x'ing.

───────────────────────────→

FIRST DATE DON'TS

Most people are very wary on first dates, always on the lookout for what's wrong with the other person—after all there must be a reason they are still single. The exception is childless women aged between 35 and 43—this demographic is absurdly positive and willing to see the good in anyone because they sense their fertility window closing and that makes them a whole lot less particular about potential mates. For the rest of us, however, any transgression, no matter how small, is usually enough to kybosh the possibility of a second date, which is why you need to be on your absolute best behaviour on that first outing. Here are some things to avoid if you are hoping to score that elusive second date.

175
One to two squirts max of perfume or aftershave

You don't want your date to smell you before they see you. Be it perfume, aftershave or Lynx deodorant, one squirt is ample, two is okay but you're pushing it. And if it happens to be the perfume Angel by Thierry Mugler, then no squirts at all is preferable. That stuff is like a biological weapon—even a single squirt is enough to render me nauseous and two squirts has me reaching for a gas mask.

176

Men, don't wear the whale tail or the shark tooth or any other pendant on a leather thong

Best to wait a few months until you've really hooked her with your sweet personality and sense of humour, then hopefully she'll find it within herself to forgive your awful man jewellery.

177

Don't be late

Nothing says your time is less valuable than mine like turning up late. On a first date, you can at least afford this new person the courtesy of being on time.

Texting that you're going to be late is still being late—your lateness is not excused because you forewarned the person of your impending lateness. Be on time.

178

Don't mention your ex

There's no good way to talk about your ex on a first date. If you are nice and positive about them, you will sound like you're still in love with them. And if you trash-talk them you will sound like you're still in love with them . . . *and* you're a bit unhinged.

179

Don't show pictures of your kids

It's too early for that. You may show pictures of your dog (as long as the dog is not wearing an outfit of any kind). And men may show pictures of their cat; however, for the ladies, while you can admit to owning a cat, you should hold off on showing any pictures of it on a first date. I know that's sexist, but I'm afraid I only make the rules, not society's attitudes.

180
Don't perform a monologue, have a conversation

A conversation is a 'turn-take' arrangement: you talk, then the other person talks. There should be at least two voices participating in a conversation. Don't relegate your date to being an audient for your monologue or your well-rehearsed 'life high-lights' package (see Conversation Rules for further clarification).

181
Don't go for dinner

I don't recommend going for dinner on a first date—there are way too many rules to think about when you're eating. Best to keep it simple and just go for a drink. Or see a movie. The movie date is an excellent first date because not only does it give you something to talk about afterwards, but it also allows you to see how the other person behaves in the cinema: you will find out immediately whether they know the rules of movie-going.

182
Don't eat the nuts or rice crackers

If the date is going well and you decide you like the person, then avoid snacking from the bowl of nuts or rice crackers on the bar. No one wants to kiss someone with nut breath or chewed-up nut paste in their teeth. And rice crackers are just as bad—they really get stuck in your teeth and, on top of that, they make your breath smell like wee.

COUPLES

183
No love on the escalator

The escalator is a thoroughfare, please don't clog it up with your public demonstrations of affection. Couples who stand side-by-side holding hands are the worst. Never ever stand two abreast. Even if you really really love your new boyfriend or girlfriend, give it a rest for the duration of the escalator ride. Stand one behind the other but resist the urge to turn yourselves into a love sculpture. Shopping centres are rife with young lovers taking advantage of the free stair ride to caress one another. Remember, it's only a temporary separation, you'll be next to one another again in less than a minute. And if you really can't take being apart for that long, then end your separation sooner by walking up or down the escalator. That's how you're supposed to use the escalator, by the way, they were designed to *assist* your journey, you're not supposed to become a human statue the minute you hit one.

184
Grocery shopping is not a romantic activity

Newly loved-up couples enjoy spending every minute together. Often for young girls going to the supermarket is a chance to play house, dragging their man through the aisles, pushing the trolley together, and fondling each other in front of the muesli as they attempt to conjure up some kind of cutesy faux-domesticity before the relationship has reached that level of familiarity. But kids, slow down, there's really no need to rush into such mundane routine behaviour, your relationship will get there soon enough and there won't be anything cutesy about it. Leave yourself somewhere to go, don't peak too early!

If you're holding hands in the supermarket, you should be at home. You're obviously still in those early stages where you're not even hungry anyway. So go home. Have sex. Order takeaway.

185
Wait at least six months before giving each other pet names

Preferably longer. There is nothing worse than someone going too early with the pet name, no matter what that pet name might be: honey, muffin, darling, love, pumpkin, sweetheart or, god forbid, 'babes'. The same goes for referring to one another as your boyfriend or girlfriend—I like to wait at least two years before I use that term, going any earlier feels like you're tempting fate.

186
Don't use the word 'lover'

It's too visual. Now we're all imagining you guys doing it. Ew.

187
No emojis when texting your partner

This is a rule I instigate when I am in a relationship. I find the use of emojis to be an extremely lazy form of communication and I think when it comes to your partner you should make an effort and do more than just 'thumbs up' them or 'smiley winky face' them. I am well aware that a lot of people will now be 'crying laughy facing' me and thinking, *Well, no wonder you're not in a relationship, lady!* And to those people I say 'poo with eyes' to you.

See, I'm not banning the use of emojis when texting, just when texting your partner. They're supposedly the most important person in your life so take the time to write out what you actually mean, even if it's just the actual words 'thumbs up, see you later'. It takes a few seconds longer, but it says you care and it's also mildly amusing, which is never a bad thing.

188
Never propose to someone in public

It puts way too much pressure on the other person to say yes.

189
If someone proposes in public, say yes even if you don't mean it

It's the kind thing to do. Later on, in private, you can take your 'yes' back and explain that you didn't want to embarrass them in public by saying no.

190
Don't fart in front of your partner

I know this is contentious. People say it's a sign of being relaxed and comfortable with your partner if you can really be yourself and, quite literally, let go in front of them. But ask yourself a few questions: Did you fart in front of them on the first date when you were trying to be impressive and sexy? Do you fart openly at work? Or at the shops? Or in restaurants? I say 'openly' because I know everyone farts; I mean, who hasn't accidentally blown off at the Lincraft counter while buying dressmaking scissors? My point is, there's a difference between sneaking one out (or being caught completely off guard by a relaxed sphincter muscle at Lincraft), and intentionally lifting your cheek and letting one rip in front of the person you, apparently, love above all others. Surely that person deserves the same amount of respect that you offer people such as work colleagues, waitstaff and shop-keeps. Familiarity breeds contempt.

191
Don't pick your nose in front of your partner

As above. A little bit of subtle digital enquiry around the edges of the nostrils is okay occasionally, but don't be plunging that finger up to the knuckle and rummaging so hard you risk punching through to your eyeballs. I'm not saying you can't pick your nose, just do it in private.

192
Never use the phrase 'Happy wife, happy life'

This phrase tends to be uttered by men who can't be arsed communicating with their partners. It's their way of saying, 'Yeah fine, whatever'. It's their way of keeping the old 'ball and chain' happy. And by keeping her happy, I mean quiet. Apparently they prefer to just nod and go along with whatever is said rather than actually listen to a woman's concerns and potentially have a spirited discussion about the issue.

193
Declare immediately that your partner is in the car with you when you answer the phone

The minute you press that speakerphone button, you must declare not only that you are in the car but that there are others present. Before the caller has a chance to speak, jump right in with: 'Hello! I'm in the car with Pete, say hello to Pete because he is right here next to me and he can hear you because we are on speakerphone, in the car, together. Pete can hear you, and I can hear you, we can both hear you . . . so, go ahead please, caller.'

194
Don't have a shared email address with your partner

Grow up guys. You are two individual people. And I should be able to write to my friend without having to worry that their spouse could also be reading my embarrassing, overthinking, girly missives.

FRIENDS OF COUPLES

195
Don't go too early with your opinion when a couple breaks up

Always wait for the couple to break up, get back together, then break up again before revealing how you really feel about the ex-partner.

ONLINE DATING RULES—FOR MEN

196
Don't list loving your kids as an attribute

This rule is really directed at divorced dads who are dating again. Tell your kids you love them by all means, as often as you like, but there's no need to tell someone you just met by dropping it into your dating profile as if it's a personality trait or a hobby. 'Hi, I'm Devon, I'm 46, I work at Macquarie Bank, I enjoy stand-up paddle boarding and I really love my kids.' These men seem to think that 'loving their kids' makes them especially great guys. But it doesn't. Loving your kids is completely normal. Of course you love your kids, you're genetically predisposed to love them, there's no need to mention it. In fact, you should love them so much that you refuse to use them as date bait. On the other hand, if you *don't* love your kids, then by all means drop that into the mix because that's completely unexpected and definitely worth discussing.

197
Don't compare yourself to James Bond

Online dating isn't supposed to be all about looks. Unlike apps such as Tinder, which are based almost exclusively on appearance, many of the dating websites purport to be less superficial, offering a chance to find out more about a person by reading their comprehensive written profile. And that's why your username is so important.

The username says a lot about you. Any woman who has tried online dating has no doubt come across countless '007's, whether it's 'Phil007' or 'IanB007'. There are also plenty of '69's—guys who like to add the suffix 69 to their username, perhaps because they were born in 1969 or more likely to let the ladies know that they are really into blow jobs. Sweet. Good to know, guys.

Obviously I'm not Beyonce and I don't speak for all the single ladies, but I would like to meet someone who puts a bit more thought into their username. Someone who takes a moment to come up with something pithy or at least mildly amusing, like SmokedMeatEnthusiast or CondimentMan.

Spend your creative energy coming up with a good username and don't bother filling out the rest—no one cares that your favourite movie is *The Shawshank Redemption* and it's news to nobody that you enjoy good food. Who doesn't like good food?

198
Use a normal photo of yourself

The best way to explain normal is by defining 'not normal'. For example:

A photo of yourself, standing shirtless in the bathroom holding your phone up to the mirror—that's not normal. You think you're showcasing your fabulous body and tempting all the laydeez with your abs, but in reality what most women see is a self-obsessed guy who takes photos of himself in the mirror.

A selection of pictures of you standing next to world-famous landmarks—that's not normal. You think it makes you look like a well-travelled gent, but in reality it makes you look like a lonely guy who went on a Contiki tour.

A photo of you wearing a suit at a wedding with a woman who has been cropped out of the photo but not completely—that's not normal. You think that by leaving just enough of her in the photo, women will note that you have dated attractive women before, which will increase your chances with other attractive women. In reality, this photo sends the subliminal message that you are a psychopath who chops things up when his girlfriend leaves him. Maybe it's just the photo of the girlfriend you chopped up or maybe it's actually the girlfriend and she's now in pieces in your freezer. I'm not saying that's what you've done, I'm just saying, that's where our minds go when we see a photo of a man with a dismembered lady's arm draped across his shoulders.

The *normal* thing to do is ask a friend to take a decent head-and-shoulders shot of you.

ONLINE DATING RULES—FOR WOMEN

199
Use a current photo

That's the most important rule. Don't use a photo that is ten years old. Or heavily filtered (unless you can filter your face in real life as well). And maybe don't have a photo of yourself jumping in the air. The number of women on dating websites who have a photo of themselves jumping into the air like they're doing a Toyota commercial leads me to believe that women have a peculiar idea of what men are looking for. I'm yet to meet a man who says to me: 'Hey lady, you look nice, but before we go for a drink, answer me this, what's your vertical leap like? Seriously, how high can you jump, from a standing start?'

200
Don't waste time filling out a profile

It's pointless, no man is ever going to do anything but look at your photo. If you must write something in the profile section, just say that you do yoga. For some reason, men think women who do yoga are going to be super-flexible and totally up for being bent over tables and contorted into all manner of weird sex-pretzel shapes.

SEX

201
If you're going to make porn, get paid for it

The internet is almost full and ninety per cent of the content is amateur porn. It's one of life's great mysteries that there are so many people out there who make videos of themselves having sex then upload it for everyone to watch. For free.

I would implore people to stop doing this. If I want to see plain doughy people having sex, I'll put a mirror on my ceiling.

202
Always take your shoes off before trying to remove jeans or pants

No matter how urgent you are to be nude, taking your shoes off first will always save you time in the long run.

203
If you tell people you are a sex therapist, expect to have to talk about it

Putting aside the fact that this job seems a bit suspect and sounds like the modern-day equivalent of those guys in the seventies who walked around wearing T-shirts that said *Sex Instructor, first lesson free!*, let's accept that sex therapist is a legitimate job. And in return, sex therapists must accept that when people discover there's a sex therapist at the dinner table, that is all anyone is going to want to talk about. No one is going to shrug and say, 'Sure, whatever, sounds dull, let's talk to Nathan, he's an actuary!' It's a bit like being a midwife—some jobs are just interesting. The difference is midwives (and nurses) usually tend to be very generous with their work stories.

Not so the sex therapist. I was at dinner once with someone who happened to be a sex therapist, and she got a bit huffy when we all took a gleeful interest in finding out exactly what her 'job' entailed, all of us peppering her with questions: 'Do you have to have sex with the person? Or do you just talk about sex?' 'Or do you watch that person having sex with someone else and call out encouragement from the sidelines like a coach?' 'What qualific-ations do you need? Is there an exam?' But instead of regaling us with fascinating tales of women whose vaginas clamp shut or men with knobs shaped like baseball bats, she looked rather put-upon, rolled her eyes and said, 'Why does everyone always want to talk about my job?'

Oh please, why do you think? Stop pretending it's not intriguing and that we should just take it in our stride. If you don't want to talk about it, don't mention it; next time tell people you are a life coach and we'll all happily leave you alone.

204
Being a sex addict is not a thing

Sex addicts only ever seem to be 'diagnosed' as such once they are busted having an affair or affairs. Until they are caught, they are just a regular person being unfaithful to their partner. But once the partner finds out about it, suddenly it's a disease and they can't help themselves. Curious.

205
Keep it down if you know there are people within earshot

It's quite possible to have sex quietly; you don't have to broad-cast your good times, especially if it's two in the morning and you're in a hotel with paper-thin walls. Have some consideration for the lonely traveller in the next room.

206
Don't refer to sex as 'being intimate' with someone

Please.

PARENTING

A word about the parenting expert

As a childless person, or barren spinster (my preferred nomen-clature), you might wonder what sort of qualifications I have to dole out parenting advice, let alone lay down actual rules for parenting. I would say that the very reason I am able to give such great advice is **because** I am childless. You see, I'm still a purist, an idealist, I have not got parenting wrong, I have not been defeated or worn down, I remain unsullied by the real-life experience of having children. That's why I'm able to tell all you parents how great it could be, if only you followed my rules.

GENERAL PARENTING RULES

207
Don't name your child after an inanimate object

Banjo. Blanket. Candlestick.

Verbs don't necessarily make great names either: Dream. Reign. Skip. Blanch. Mash.

And you should definitely think twice before you name your child after cheese: Cheddar. Wensleydale. Buffalo Mozzarella. Even Brie only works if you can guarantee the kid is going to grow up to be really, really good looking.

208
Birth videos should only be viewed by the people who made the baby

Film the birth of your child if you must but don't have a screening for your friends, no matter how dear those friends are. And definitely don't horrify your other children by showing it to them either. Sure, childbirth is a beautiful, amazing, natural thing but no one needs to bear witness to exactly how wide that hole can go.

209
It's not babysitting if they are your children

This is a common bugbear for a lot of mothers. For some reason, fathers will often refer to staying home to look after their own children as 'babysitting', as if it's some sort of chore rather than an inherent part of being a parent.

210
Do not negotiate with children

When you give in to a child's demands, it creates a precedent, and guarantees more hijackings of family outings and even more insane demands in future.

211
Boobs yes, Bugaboos no

Breastfeeding mothers, you are welcome in cafes, restaurants, kiosks; wherever you want to get your nourishers out is absolutely fine. Nobody cares. If we're staring at you, it's only because we're trying to work out the right way to salute you for being such amazing people and giving life to a new generation. We don't even care if you bring your toddler into the cafe and spend a stupid amount of money on a teeny-tiny cup of frothy milk that your child adoringly refers to as a 'bubbycheemo' (oh bless). Points to you for keeping the economy buoyant.

The thing people object to about mothers in cafes is when you gather en masse and choke the place up with a cluster of those giant Bugaboo prams. Like you're a bunch of cowboys circlin' the wagons and gittin' ready for a shoot-out. Two prams max inside per group. Even then, one is preferable. Spare a thought for the poor waitstaff who have to negotiate their way around these hazards while carrying hot beverages. If the group has multiple prams, why not get takeaway coffees and go to the park instead? Kids prefer the park, they really do.

212
Your child's snot is your responsibility

When you see it, wipe it. Without delay. During the early years, your child is still a strange hybrid creature, half human/half petri dish. But you can't expect a child to care about having what is essentially an open-cut mine of disease streaming out of their nostrils. That's why you, as the parent, are responsible for whisking that snot away as quickly as possible before it can be transferred onto anyone or anything else.

213
No bare bums on tables

It is, of course, an absolute outrage when a cafe doesn't provide a change table in the bathroom and you should definitely take that up with management or perhaps call Tracy Grimshaw and have one of her *ACA* journalists barge into that establishment with cameras and shout aggressively at the owner about why they hate children and why they think mothers are second-class citizens who don't deserve equal rights. But just because the cafe is disrespecting you by not having a change table, it doesn't mean you have the right to punish all the other innocent diners with the sight of your child's bumhole being lifted and wiped on a table right next to where they are eating.

214
Childless people reserve the right to be both petrified of and disgusted by nits

As a parent, you are obliged to deal with these revolting and terrifying parasites in a rational and non-alarmist fashion. It's your job, it's what you signed up to do when you had a kid. In return you receive unconditional love from your child and, if you play your cards right, someone to look after you when you get old and infirm.

Childless people receive none of these benefits or rewards, which is why we are compensated by living in a world without small creatures that bring home even smaller microscopic creatures crawling all over them. So don't roll your eyes and 'tsk' at us when we freak out and refuse to come over to your place when your kid has nits. Or worms. Or school sores. Or whooping cough and measles if you live in the Byron Shire—which, considering the low vaccination rate, should really think about changing its name to Ground Zero.

215
Don't put your child on the phone to 'say hello'

Children are not great on the phone; if you work hard enough you can extract a few single-word answers from them but most of the time you just listen to them huff and breathe into the phone like a creepy stalker. Even when you are the child's owner it can be hard to get more than a few words out of them. I've heard many people struggling to keep a 'conversation' going with their own child but I guess, as a parent, you don't mind so much because you simply enjoy hearing every precious breath your child takes. But for the rest of us, we've got stuff we could be getting on with. The exception, of course, is grandma. If I was a parent, I'd make calling grandma a daily event, I'd say a quick hello then whack my kid on the phone with Grammy while I hustled off to get a few jobs done. Old person and young child on the phone are like cheese and chutney—the perfect combination; one likes to natter and the other just makes an occasional breathing noise to assure you that there is actually someone 'listening' at the other end.

216
Reserve the phrase 'good job' for something worthwhile

Children get accolades for the most basic of tasks these days. When they sit down at the dinner table it's 'good job, sweetie'. If they flush the toilet it's 'good job, Tilly'. Even the act of taking their cup to the sink elicits a 'good job, Xander'. I'm worried this might make life difficult for children when they get older and enter the workforce. All this 'good-jobbing' could make them confused and needy. I imagine they'll be sitting at their desk on their first day wondering why a co-worker didn't say 'good job' for drinking their coffee without spilling it or why the boss hasn't 'good-jobbed' them for arriving on time and sitting up straight. Let's reward them with 'good job' when they do something genuinely useful, like mow the lawn or retile the bathroom.

217
Don't climb Mount Everest if you have children under eighteen

When you have children, you are obliged to try to stay alive for them at least until they reach adulthood. Climbing Mount Everest is a pointlessly dangerous endeavour. I say pointless because it's not a mountain that needs to be conquered. It's already been conquered. Many times over. And filing up the mountain in your expensive climbing gear while someone else carries your oxygen and everything else you need to survive is not really proving anything, except perhaps that you have a lot of money.

Consider the fact that Sir Edmund Hillary already did it over sixty years ago wearing little more than a smart woollen jumper and a parka, and there are Sherpas who run up and down that thing several times a day wearing not much more than a beanie and underpants.

Do your kids a favour and don't die unnecessarily for the sake of winning Instagram for a few weeks.

PREGNANCY

218
Maternity photo shoots are not compulsory

Pregnancy photos are becoming as overblown and portentous as wedding photos. All you need is one good shot every couple of months to document a pregnancy. It doesn't need to be a major production. Enough with the Demi Moore-style naked shots with the 'hand bra' and the leg stepped forward to conceal the minge. No more wistful cradling of the tum-tum. And let's ban 'heart hands' on bellies. I'm more than happy to see you photographed while pregnant, I just want to see something new. Oh and remember, you don't have to be naked. I can still see that you're pregnant when you have clothes on. (Having said that, hats off to Amy Schumer for running naked in ugg boots through Central Park for her pregnancy shoot. That was funny.)

219
You don't have to call it a 'belly'

It can still be a stomach. For some reason everyone feels obliged to call it a 'belly' when they're pregnant.

220
Pregnant women are not magic lamps—don't rub them

Always ask first. Or better yet, wait for the pregnant woman herself to suggest the idea—but don't be surprised, or annoyed, if she doesn't. Not everyone likes their tummy rubbed. (My dog can't believe I just said that.)

221
Keep pregnancy announcements simple

There's a growing trend for people to announce their second child by photographing their first child holding up the ultrasound of the new baby—which is really off-putting because it kind of looks like your toddler is pregnant.

222
Gender-reveal parties are not a thing

If you were thinking about having one of these, don't. Just have dinner with your friends and tell them you're having a boy or a girl. That's all anyone needs; in fact, I don't even need that, I'm happy to wait until the baby is born and have a look for myself.

SPECIAL SEALED SECTION
FOR MUMS

I am aware I am not a mother. However, I do have a mother, so I know what they're like. These rules are for mothers everywhere.

———————————————————————→

223
Calling something 'delicious' does not make it so

Mothers have an odd habit of thinking they can trick children into eating something simply by referring to it as 'delicious'. My mum still does it today.

'Would you like a slice of this delicious spelt loaf?'

'No thanks, Mum, I'd like a slice of bread that tastes like bread but hey, you go ahead and tuck into that "delicious" loaf made of grass and cement.'

224
Don't fixate on irrelevant details

If your teenager is talking to you, you need to act casual—be interested but not too interested, just let them tell the story and take what you're given. Do not, however, frighten them off by peppering them with specific questions.

My mother, for example, always wanted to know about the numbers; she was obsessed with how many people were present at any party I went to. Yes, she was interested in knowing who was there, but mostly she wanted to know how many were there. I don't know why. I'm sure she thought I was being recalcitrant when I shrugged and said 'I dunno' every time she asked but, the thing is, I genuinely did not know. I still don't. To this day, once the number of people goes above eight, I'm clueless. Could be ten, could be sixty-three, could be four score and seven. I have no idea. I am the opposite of Rainman. And whenever I watch Dustin Hoffman in that scene where the waitress drops the box of toothpicks and then Ray correctly identifies exactly how many are on the floor in a matter of seconds—'246, 246 toothpicks total, 246'—I think about my mum and how happy she would have been if only I'd had those kind of skills.

'How many people were at the party?'

'246, 246 people at the party, Mom, 246 total, 246.'

225
Don't chase children with food

No one will die if they leave the house without breakfast. There's no need to pursue your child down the street waving a banana and trying to stuff it into their bag as they attempt to get away from you.

226
Keep a packet of fresh tissues to hand

Mothers are always being asked for tissues. Always. And yet for some reason, they can never produce a fresh one. Admittedly they can always produce a tissue, of sorts. Usually some screwed up, lint-covered rag they've fished out of the bottom of their handbag, one that they insist is clean as they unball it and smooth it out while handing it to you. If you're a mum, you know that someone at some point during the day is going to need a tissue, so when you're grabbing your essentials—keys, purse, phone—why not grab a little packet of unused tissues and throw them in your bag too.

227
Don't use inappropriate analogies

Does your child really treat the place like a hotel? And if so, is that such a bad thing? Every hotel I've ever been to takes my credit card up front and I'm then held liable for all expenses.

Maybe you should start treating the place like a hotel too, and charging them for everything from housekeeping to meals served in the hotel restaurant—or, as you probably call it, your kitchen.

Does their bedroom *really* look like a brothel? Have you ever walked in to find a fat sweaty man with his pants around his ankles and a bored-looking woman trying to act sexy while she digs around in a big bowl of condoms beside the bed? Or is the room just a bit messy? My guess is brothel workers keep their rooms quite tidy. I certainly don't imagine they have wet towels dumped all over the floor, piles of clothes on top of the bed, plus a dirty old bong and countless used cups and plates pushed under the bed; the bed is a workspace, after all—it's probably kept clear of all clutter. So let's not insult the sex workers by comparing them to your slovenly teenagers.

228
Stop wasting fruit

That's what you're doing every time you put an apple or an orange or a banana into a lunchbox. Save yourself some time and just put that thing straight in the bin—that's where it's going eventually. The only uncertainty is whether it's going to happen at school on the day or at home three weeks later when it's exhumed in a blackened and slimy state from the bottom of their school bag.

229
Don't ask your child if they will be warm enough

They don't know. They don't care. They don't have an answer. You're pissing into the wind with this one.

CHILDREN'S PARTIES

230
You don't have to invite the whole class

Seriously, it's okay to leave some kids out. Similarly, it's okay if your child is sometimes left out. We can't all be friends with everyone. It's unrealistic.

231
Don't waste money on gifts children won't appreciate

Chances are the first birthday a child will actually remember is their fourth birthday, so keep the money you would have spent on gifts for those first few birthdays and put it towards their education. I'm kidding, who cares about that? Take the money you would have spent on those first few birthdays and buy something nice for yourself instead. You deserve it. The kid will be just as happy with a roll of bubble wrap or a box of those foam packing peanuts. In fact, I know a three-year-old boy who desperately wanted a box of surgical gloves for his birthday. It cost his mum $3.99 and he has never been happier. Your kids will become an enormous and endless financial drain soon enough, so conserve money while you can.

232
No smash cakes

If you haven't heard of smash cakes, then please head to Facebook and post about how 'hashtag blessed' you are because I certainly wish I had never heard of them. A smash cake is exactly what it sounds like: a cake that parents with too much money buy for their child to 'smash'. Oftentimes they also hire a photographer to document this wanton destruction because who doesn't want a picture of a toddler covered head to toe in cake. Soy cyute.

233
One prize only in pass the parcel

Pass the parcel used to be a game that had you on tenterhooks. As the parcel went around, each layer came off, the parcel got smaller and you got ever closer to the prize within. Sometimes you would go to a party where the parent had got real fancy and tucked a Mintie or a Fantale into an occasional layer. Not every layer, just randomly throughout—it really kept the kids on edge, all that anticipation and not knowing made for a surprisingly exciting game. These days, all the tension has gone and pass the parcel is not so much a game anymore but rather a group unwrapping exercise. Every layer contains a prize of equal value. The parent makes sure the music stops on a different kid each time (fair enough, I won't legislate against that) and everyone gets a prize. It's pointless and unfun.

PETS

Putting rules for pets in the parenting section might seem offensive to some, but I gave it serious consideration and came to the conclusion that owning a pet and owning a toddler aren't really that different. There's a lot of cleaning up after them, a lot of stopping them from putting random objects in their mouths, a lot of rejecting other people's opinions on how to make them behave, and an awful lot of apologising if they bite someone at day care.

234
Pick up your dog's poo

Once again, I start with the obvious. This is a genuine problem in dog parks where dogs are off the lead. You need to watch your dog like a hawk when he's off the lead, lest he run off and do a poo somewhere and you don't witness it. There's no philosophical debate about dog poo. It's not like when that tree falls in the forest and possibly makes no sound because no one is there to hear it. When a dog poos in the park, even if there's nobody around to see it, that poo still hits the ground, it still smells and it still needs to be picked up, post-haste, by you, before someone steps in it.

235
Don't stand around talking at the dog park

Keep it moving people, keep it moving, circulate, walk those dogs. When people cluster, dogs cluster, and that's when fights start—between both the dogs and the people. Seriously, there is way too much spurious advice being doled out at the dog park by enthusiastic amateurs who have watched a few episodes of *The Dog Whisperer* and now fancy themselves as professional dog trainers. Dog training is like parenting—unless someone asks you specifically for your opinion, best to keep it to yourself.

236
Never presume your animal is acting out of spite

Dogs don't chew your stuff or piss on the rug in order to get revenge. Spite is not in your dog's emotional repertoire. There is simply no such thing as a dog (or a cat) doing a 'spite wee'. If your pet is pissing on things or chewing things, he might be anxious or bored or agitated by something but he's not being spiteful. Unless of course the animal is a hamster—those things are positively biblical in their quest for vengeance.

237
Dogs don't speak English

You have to teach a dog English, just like you would a toddler. You can't just get a puppy and say 'sit sit sit sit sit' and expect him to know what that means. As for complex sentences, like 'Baxter, be nice, be gentle, remember when you were a puppy, Baxter, you didn't like it when big dogs jumped on you, so be nice please!' Guess what? Baxter didn't get any of that.

238
If your dog does something wrong, apologise

It's mortifying when your dog does something wrong—whether he's aggressive towards another dog or jumps on a child or steals a sandwich out of a kid's sports bag or, in my dog's case, pisses on a lady in a fancy hat sitting in the park enjoying the sunshine. When these things happen, don't try to excuse or justify the behaviour: 'Oh I'm sorry, he really doesn't like black and white dogs' or 'Sorry, he's a bit frightened of skateboards' or 'Sorry, he really enjoys pissing on people in hats.' Just apologise unreservedly—'I'm so sorry my dog pissed on you'—put your dog back on the leash and walk away.

239
Never say you hate cats if you haven't had a cat

How do you know? You can still say you prefer dogs but don't say you hate cats. There is nothing hateable about a cat. And you'd know that if you'd ever had one.

240
There should never be more than one poo in a litter tray

Your house does not have to stink just because you have a cat. I watch a lot of that show *My Cat from Hell* on the Animal Planet channel and I see many people who claim that their cat goes to the toilet outside the tray. But when the cat-whisperer guy visits, you see that the litter trays are chock full of poo?! Well, no wonder the cat started crapping outside the box?! What cat wants to stand on top of a pile of poo in order to do another poo. Empty the litter tray every time there's a poo in it. Every time.

FASHION

A word about fashion

It's a brave person who dispenses fashion advice. Fashion updates more often than my stupid phone's software and my stupid phone's software needs updating all the time. (Which I really don't understand—why can't they get it right the first time?)

Over the years, I have committed many fashion errors and indeed a few crimes. The most serious of these occurred when I was just ten years old. I went out, in public, to a restaurant wearing grey corduroy knickerbockers teamed with a matching grey flannel shirt that buttoned up down one side and had a high-neck ruffled collar—kind of House of Tudor meets frill-neck lizard. The occasion was my tenth birthday and Mum had taken me shopping for a special birthday outfit to wear to my birthday dinner at The Black Stump—which, in my mind, was the fanciest restaurant in town. Was there anything more sophisticated than a chewy, well-done steak (I was young, I didn't *know any better, that's how I requested it be cooked) and one of those delicious baked potatoes in foil that came accompanied by the famous Black Stump condiment caddy of sour cream, chives and cubes of butter?*

For some reason I decided the most appropriate way to dress for this sophisticated occasion was to dress like Prince —
if Prince's favourite colour had been grey and if he'd chosen to be a parking inspector rather than a fabulously purple, music industry demigod.

I guess what I'm pointing out here is that I am possibly not the right person to be dispensing rules about fashion. But then again, one of my most important rules for life is: 'Do as I say, not as I do.'

GENERAL FASHION RULES

241
All buttons on or below the nipline must be done up

The simplest way to know whether a button should be done up or can be left undone is to draw an imaginary line across your chest from nipple to nipple—that's the 'nipline'—and any button that sits on or below that line should be done up. It's not 1977.

242
Team jerseys are not for going out in

A woman wouldn't wear a Wing Defence bib to a nightclub, so men should apply the same standards and eschew the footy jerseys and NBA singlets when it comes to selecting clothes for a night out.

243
No shoe mash-ups

Ever since German physicist Albert Klochwireless successfully combined the clock and the radio in 1932, humans have been desperate to mash things together, largely without success. The mocha is one such example, combining two perfectly satisfactory stand-alone beverages into one unpleasant drink that doesn't taste quite right. Is it a coffee that tastes a bit like chocolate? Or is it a hot chocolate that tastes a bit like shit?

Some of the more recent mash-ups come courtesy of the shoe world. The particular shoe mongrel that comes to mind is the high-heeled sneaker. A completely pointless piece of footwear.

What you have is a sneaker that is no longer comfortable—which, when you think about it, is the sneaker's greatest attribute. And a high heel that is no longer elegant—which is easily the high heel's *only* attribute.

The boot sandal is another strange shoe hybrid that keeps popping up—all the trappings of a boot but with the toe and the heel cut out, rendering it inappropriate footwear for both winter and summer.

244
Wear socks

Unless you're wearing sandals (or thongs) you should be wearing socks. It's really a question of hygiene. When I see a man wearing shoes with no socks, I don't think, *Ooh, that's a tidy ankle, what a treat to get a peek at that exposed joint!* I think, *Oh man, there is some serious fungus being harvested in those shoes.*

245
Keep your socks age-appropriate

Some people find the current 'Happy Socks' trend offensive, especially when it's middle-aged men parading around in super-fun socks covered in cat faces and pineapples. Personally, I don't care what socks you wear, as long as you wear socks.

246
Forty-dollar rubber thongs are the same as two-dollar rubber thongs

Spend your money elsewhere. Perhaps on a delicious sherry vinegar—which happens to be my favourite of all the vinegars.

247
No one looks good in Hammer Pants

Hammer Pants are so named because they originally came to our attention when they were worn by the rapper MC Hammer, who was what I like to call a gentleman rapper. He was around back in the day when rappers mostly referred to women as 'ladies' and 'fly girls' as opposed to the present day where we are all 'bitches' and 'hos'.

The distinguishing feature of the Hammer Pant is the ridiculously low-slung, baggy crutch. They are large and billowy around the thigh area but they tighten around the calf and ankle. The more accurate name for these pants is 'poo-catchers' because it really does look like you have mistaken your pants for a toilet. And after that description, you'd be forgiven for wondering why I have even brought them up. Surely Hammer Pants are dead and gone, never to be seen again, except perhaps on *Rage* late at night during a special early nineties, 'Gentlemen of Rap' edition featuring Mr Hammertime, Young MC, Tone Loc, et al.

But no. For some inexplicable reason, every ten years or so they rise again, appearing in fashion magazines, where they are worn by impossibly thin, beautiful models leaning against rocks by the sea or standing astride vintage bicycles. These waifs make the pants look not only super-comfy but somehow elegant, too—fooling the rest of us into thinking, *Hmm, perhaps I do need some of those pants for next time I go to the coast and want to lean against rocks . . .* Don't be fooled. When it comes to Hammer Pants, remember the words of the very wise MC Hammer himself and don't touch them.

FASHION FOR THE OVER-FORTIES

248
Don't buy your entire wardrobe from Kathmandu

Or Mountain Designs or any of those other outdoorsy stores. Sure, the clothes are comfortable and they are very well serviced by a ridiculous number of pockets, but the truth is you're going to Balmoral for fish and chips by the harbour, not Base Camp 1.

249
Ladies, avoid anything too 'fun' in the fashion department

Tops with applique or sequins are extremely difficult to pull off once you reach about forty. Young people get away with wearing them because it's ironic and kooky to dress like their crazy old aunt. Once you're forty, however, you just look like the crazy old aunt. But hang in there because ...

250
Once you hit sixty, all bets are off

At sixty, suddenly you *are* the crazy old aunt and now is the time to break out the bedazzler and start styling up your denim jacket or your waistcoat or even an old windcheater. Get creative with beads and glitter, get yourself a Spotlight store account and, while you're at it, find some brightly coloured tapered trousers because you are officially a fun old bat. It's good times ahead as you see out your senior years in a riot of colour and craft.

251
The older you get, the less denim you should wear

Between forty and forty-five is a good time to start thinking about alternatives to jeans. Especially if you're a man. You don't have to give them up completely just yet, but perhaps start phasing them out, because once you hit retirement age you need to give up wearing jeans altogether. Coincidentally there is a new Coen brothers film coming out about this exact problem, it's called *No Jeans for Old Men*.

252
If you look like a rolled roast, go up a size

I used to be a size 8 but I'm not anymore. However, after years of reaching for the same size, it's a hard habit to break. And there's no question, I'm in slight denial about my increase in girth, so a lot of the time I still try to pour myself into a size 8. Invariably it's way too tight, it grips me in all the wrong places, and highlights every lump, bump and fat roll. It really does look like I've been trussed around the midsection with butcher's twine. Time to go up a size and be comfortable.

DENIM AND LEATHER

253
Denim is for jeans and jackets

Not slacks or coats.

254
Only really hot people can wear double denim

Life is unfair sometimes.

255
Leather pants are best avoided

The window for wearing leather pants is even more elusive than the one where a pear becomes just ripe enough to eat but not so ripe that it becomes mushy. It's somewhere between the ages of nineteen and twenty-one—but even if you're the right age, that's still no guarantee you can pull off leather pants.

Leather pants are difficult to wear both literally and figuratively. They are physically very heavy and they don't have a lot of give, which makes them hard to get on and off. Once on, they don't breathe. At all. And forget about 'wicking' properties. Any sweat you produce inside those leather pants is staying in there till you get them off and wipe them clean. On top of that, you have to be the perfect size. Long-haired ladies in leather pants who are too thin risk being mistaken for the lead singer of an eighties cock-rock band. Yet anyone even slightly larger than a size zero risks being mistaken for a couch.

SPECIAL SEALED SECTION
TATTOOS

*The following section has been sealed because it's for cleanskins only. There's no point in tattooed folk reading these rules, you've already gone and drawn on yourselves. I'm curious to see whether Generation Z and the current crop of youth will reject tattoos when they get older. In the world they inhabit, everyone from their spinster aunt to their grandad to their daggy geography teacher has tatts and surely that makes them predictable and conformist. Perhaps in the future, **not** getting a tattoo will be seen as a rebellious act.*

⟶

256
No tattoos above your collarbone

If I have to explain why you shouldn't tattoo your neck and face,
I can't help you. Put the book down and walk away.

257
Don't get a tattoo because you lost a bet

Far better to be known as a welcher than the idiot who got a
stupid tattoo. People will quickly forget that you lost a bet about
who could eat the hottest curry (which is such a dumb bet—why
do men think it's so great to be able to eat really spicy food?),
but no one can forget that pointless tattoo of a red chilli that
you now have on your shoulder forever. A badly drawn chilli that
looks more like an angry pointy penis with a strange bend in it.

258
No tribe? No tattoo for you

If you choose to get 'inked' with tribal tattoos, you must be able
to prove your affiliation with said tribe plus give the full history
of that tribe and the specific cultural significance of each of the
tattoos you have selected.

259
No butterfly or dolphin tattoos

This is because as your body sags and spreads you'll soon find
yourself sporting a dirty old moth in place of the butterfly, and
where you once had a majestic dolphin leaping across your deltoid
now there's a sad, lumpy creature that looks more like a dugong.

260
Decide on your tattoo, then wait a year

Then if you still believe it's a good idea, wait one more year. Better to be safe than sorry you got stuck with something you thought was cool in your twenties.

If I'd been tattooed back in the day, I might now be a middle-aged lady with a tramp stamp of the Bear surfboard logo from *Big Wednesday* across my lower back or a vague likeness of Neil from *The Young Ones* besmirching my calf. And there's no doubt that the Neil 'portrait' would have been one of those heavily shaded 'famous person' tattoos you see that makes you do a double take because at first glance, it looks like Marilyn Monroe (or Elvis or James Dean or whoever) was actually black?!

The 'wait a year' rule is even more important if you are thinking about getting a written statement tattooed on yourself. I guarantee you the Bra Boys have now realised that everyone already knows 'Blood is thicker than water' and that it's not the incredible revelation they originally thought it to be. It's a bit like having 'Sea water is undrinkable' or 'It gets harder to lose weight as you get older' tattooed around your neck—some things just don't need to be said. Especially in permanent ink on your person.

261
Never have someone's face tattooed on your knee

It might seem like the perfect spot when you're younger—after all, it's round and face-shaped! But as you age, so too will the person you have immortalised on your knee and eventually they'll start to look like they are stroking out.

262
Never have someone's knee tattooed on your face

To be fair, this is not something I've ever seen before, I just thought I'd try to get ahead of the curve and make a pre-emptive rule.

PIERCINGS AND OTHER HOLES

263
Maximum two piercings per head

Please choose wisely.

264
Don't make large holes in your ears

Ten years ago, no one would have believed we would ever need a rule to stop people from stretching their earlobes to the point where you can stick your fists through them. A special note to any kids thinking about getting these: it's not like piercing your ears. The gaping holes you've created will not simply close over and heal themselves, you will need surgery to repair them. So if you must pay tribute to the traditions of the Maasai, perhaps think about shaving your head or wearing a fetching red robe. They also drink a lot of milk-based beverages and wear beautiful beaded jewellery. I'm just saying there are plenty of less permanent ways to appropriate someone else's culture.

SUNGLASSES

265
Sunglasses are for outside

The clue is in the word: sunglasses are glasses that protect your eyes from the sun. So unless you are Corey Hart, you don't need to wear them at night, and unless you're Stevie Wonder, you don't need to wear them inside.

266
Don't stow your sunglasses on the back of your neck

Either take them off and put them away when you no longer need them or pop them on top of your head. But never on the back of your neck. Queensland men appear to be the main offenders when it comes to 'backnecking' sunglasses, with the Gold Coast in particular being the backneck crime capital of the world.

267
Sunglasses are not a wig

This is a special rule for bald men. Wearing sunglasses atop your head does not hide your hairlessness; we all still know you're bald.

MAKEUP

268
Ladies, go easy with the contouring

Contouring is something the Kardashians introduced to the main-stream; however, it is also something best left to professional makeup artists. Applied expertly, contouring can subtly change the appearance of your face by shading certain areas—it can draw attention away from a double chin or correct a bumpy nose or give you sharply defined cheekbones where once you had none.

Unfortunately, these days most contouring is being done with the heavy hand of an enthusiastic amateur, which is why we are seeing a lot of gals contouring themselves so excessively that they start to resemble an extra in the *Lion King* musical or Rum Tum Tugger from *Cats*.

269
Big false eyelashes look like big false eyelashes

You are fooling no one with those thick, heavy, fake, stick-on lashes. There's not a single person looking at you thinking, *Wow, that woman's eyelashes are amazing!* Rather, we are all thinking, *Jesus, how is she managing to keep her eyes open with those giant black tentacles glued to her lids?*

270
Less is more

This is an all ages rule. When you are young, your skin is youthful and dewy, there's no need to put a thick coat of paint on it.

And when you are older, it's even more important to back off—especially around the eyes—lest you start looking like a crepey old drag queen or Lesley Joseph in *Birds of a Feather.*

Drag queens (and Lesley Joseph) you are the exceptions to this rule; obviously, you guys can go nuts.

271
Leave your eyebrows alone

There is quite the trend at the moment for stencilled eyebrows. Where once, drawn-on eyebrows were the purview of old ladies whose eyebrows had fallen out over the years, now more and more young people are choosing to Frida Kahlo themselves with a pair of heavy, drawn-on eyebrows.

The obvious problem with this is that you need to decide in the morning on your mood for the day. Should you draw on a pair of angry eyebrows? Or maybe surprised eyebrows? Or perhaps you fancy that you'll be spending a large part of your day making wry comments that require you to have one eyebrow raised while the other stays put.

The best solution to this conundrum is to put the crayon down and leave your eyebrows alone.

272
Never trust a woman in a lab coat at the makeup counter

You see these ladies in department stores all the time but, remember, the white coat is a total misdirect—this woman is neither scientist nor makeup artist. She is simply a sales assistant who likes to 'have fun with makeup' (and she probably stole that coat from the Ponds Institute). As such, she is not to be trusted. If you do get sucked in and decide to sit down and let her do your makeup, be prepared to walk around for the rest of the day resembling Nanki-Poo from *The Mikado*.

MODELS

273
Models don't get to say that they were
ugly or unattractive at school

Sorry, but no one believes you. Nor do we think it's upsetting that you were apparently 'bullied' by kids who called you 'lanky' or 'Giraffe'. Neither of these things is particularly insulting. You can't undo the fact that you won the gene lottery, just go with it.

Oh and we don't believe that you 'pig out' on burgers and fries either. Because if you did you'd look like the rest of us.

AT THE MOVIES

A word about the cinema

Years ago I met an English comedian named Ian in the dressing room of the London Comedy Store. He was quite possibly the most stylish man I had ever encountered, certainly on the comedy scene, where comedians (straight ones anyway) aren't exactly known for their sartorial elegance. Ian was a mod. He was tidy and unbelievably well dressed: he looked like he'd just stepped out of the pages of a 1969 magazine called Mod Style Monthly *or* Piss Elegant Gents. *What I remember most about Ian, however, was the fact that he hadn't been to the cinema in twenty years.*

At first, when he told me that, I didn't believe him —I thought he was doing a bit but he wasn't. For a start he wasn't that type of comic, he didn't do bits at you in dressing rooms (which was another reason to like him), but also he happened to be telling the truth. He said that he found it too tense to watch films in the company of complete strangers, whose behaviour you had no control over.

He told me the last time he had gone to the movies, all those years ago, it had ended very badly. A fellow cinema-goer sitting behind him wouldn't stop talking. Ian shushed him numerous times but the man would not be shushed. So Ian punched him. It's the sort of thing we all feel like doing but (fortunately) no one actually does it.

*Being an otherwise reasonable man, Ian realised immediately that he couldn't just go around punching people because that is not how a civilised society works. However, he also realised that he couldn't **not** punch someone who kept talking during a movie. His rather extreme solution was to simply stop going to the movies. I adored his conviction. Twenty years! That's a long time.*

Ian now lives with his wife and three children in the French countryside where he is easily the best-dressed farmer the world has ever seen. It's approaching forty years since he has been to the cinema and therefore I would like to dedicate the following section to him.

FOR MOVIE-GOERS

274
No talking once the previews start

Low-volume talking through the ads is permitted but once the previews start, stop talking. The previews should be seen as an extension of the movie and, of course, we all know there is no talking during the movie. I haven't written that as a rule because I think it's actually the law and if it isn't it should be—there should be cinema police who arrest people for talking during the movie.

275
Wait and let the story unfold

If you can't understand what's going on, chances are it will become apparent in time, just be patient. There's nothing worse than when a new character appears on screen and someone says, 'Who's that?' or 'What's he doing?' Hey! No one knows yet, they just appeared, let the story unfold.

276
Support the lone shusher

If someone in the cinema has the courage to shush the chatter, then be sure to add your endorsement with a loud 'Yes! Shush!' or even a 'Hear, hear!' I wouldn't normally advocate using 'hear, hear' outside of the British Parliament in the 1600s but it's dark in the cinema, no one will see you. It's really important to back up the shusher; they are showing real courage and also performing an essential service. They're like the First Responders of cinema.

277
Avoid noisy snacks in crinkly packets

If you must munch crisps during a movie (and I wish you wouldn't, but if you must), then rip the bag open quickly. Don't do that thing where you laboriously prise it open millimetre by millimetre, you're just prolonging the agony. Rip that bandaid off and get on with your infernal crunching.

278
Turn your phone off

Please note the exact wording of this rule, which is turn your phone *off*. Recently cinemas have lowered their standards and the pre-movie announcement now requests, very politely, that you turn your phone to silent. However, if it's only on silent, you'll be tempted to keep checking it throughout the film. And when you check your phone in the cinema, the screen lights you up like a lone streetlamp on a dark country road and irritates anyone within a six-seat radius. So turn it off, sit back and enjoy the film uninterrupted.

Nothing will happen in that ninety minutes that can't wait until you leave the cinema. And if, god forbid, something life-shatteringly awful *does* happen, isn't it better that you got to enjoy that last ninety minutes completely worry-free, especially now that your life has taken a complete turn for the worse?

279
Leave a courtesy buffer seat

Unless the movie is completely sold out, never take the seat immediately next to someone else. Always leave at least one or two seats between you and the next punter.

I go to the movies by myself a fair bit (admittedly it's not always my choice, a lot of people refuse to go anywhere with me because of all my rules) and, when I do go alone, I like to have what I call a 'seat moat' all around me. Imagine me in my seat, with three free seats in front of me, one empty seat either side and then three more empty ones behind me. A perfect ring of personal space all around. That's the dream.

280
Movie then dinner, never dinner then a movie

This is really just common sense. If you go to dinner first, you'll be clock-watching throughout your meal and potentially rushing your food in order to make it to the movie on time.

More importantly, however, seeing the movie first gives you something to talk about over dinner. Ideal for a first date, when you don't really know each other, but also perfect for a couple who have been together for a long time. Being able to discuss the movie saves you from looking like that couple who have run out of things to say to one another and whose sole job it is now to sit in restaurants and depress other couples who look across at you and think, *Shit, I hope we don't become that couple,* or *Shit, I wonder how long before we become that couple?*

SPECIAL SEALED SECTION
POPCORN

If you have read my previous book you will already know that I have a lot of completely irrational and totally unenforceable rules about popcorn. I am very much aware that these rules make me seem like a real nut-job, which is why I have metaphorically sealed this particular section. Consider this an appendix for serious rule enthusiasts only.

———————————————————→

281
Don't eat popcorn at the cinema

If I had my way, popcorn would be banned from cinemas. I actually like popcorn but I don't think it should be eaten in confined
windowless spaces such as movie theatres. Commercially produced
popcorn stinks far more than the popcorn you make for yourself at home. The artificial stench of over-heated oil and rancid
butter flavouring is nauseating and there's no escaping it at the
movies. The noxious popcorn miasma hits you the minute you
walk into the foyer and it gets even worse once you sit down
in the actual cinema—because the only thing more offensive
than the smell of popcorn is the smell of masticated popcorn.
And that's exactly what you get when a room full of people sit in
the dark and chomp away on that stuff with their mouths open.

282
You don't need a giant wastepaper basket full of popcorn

Just get a small one. The large ones are stupidly large. It's physically impossible to eat that much popcorn because your face
can't cope with that amount of salt. Your mouth starts to pucker
and it gets harder and harder to push each kernel through what
has become a very restricted opening between your shrivelled
up lips. That's usually the time you put your enormous bucket
of popcorn under your seat, promptly forget about it and then
kick it over when you get up to leave. It then gets ground into
the carpet and the popcorn-stink cycle is complete.

This rule is especially relevant for parents taking kids to
the movies. A small popcorn is ample; there is nothing worse
than seeing a kid with a box of popcorn bigger than its head.

Sometimes they can't even see past the popcorn to watch the movie properly.

On top of all that, there's the outrageous cost. Popcorn costs about ten cents to make and yet cinemas charge you half a week's wages for a box of it. When you add that to the price of a movie ticket, it's surprising that anyone can still afford to go to the cinema in this country. At the risk of sounding like a Mum's Handy Hint website, I suggest being more organised and buying all your popcorn and snacks at the supermarket before you get to the cinema. It will not only save you money, but if everyone starts doing it cinemas might eventually realise no one is buying their hot smelly popcorn and get rid of it.

283
The handful of popcorn must be smaller than your mouth

Don't take large fistfuls of popcorn and push and shove them into your mouth like a toddler forcing a square peg into a round hole. If popcorn is spilling back into the feed-bucket or onto your lap and the floor around you, then you're taking too much. I realise it's dark and no one can see, but that's no reason to suddenly start eating like a bulimic possum. Slow down, take smaller 'handfuls' and chew. With your mouth closed, obviously.

284
Get a choc-top instead

My ideal movie snack is the plain vanilla choc-top. Once opened, it doesn't make much noise and you've almost always finished it by the time the movie starts anyway. And if you're at a good cinema, you can also enjoy a nice glass of red wine. If the cinema you're frequenting doesn't serve wine, or they serve it in plastic cups, find a better cinema. Quality cinemas are easily identified. All you need to do is ask three simple questions:

1. *Do you serve wine in stemware?* The answer should be 'yes, of course'.
2. *Do you screen movies with Rob Schneider in them?* The answer should be 'no, of course not'.
3. *Do you have a Gold Class section?* That's when they should hang up on you, too insulted to be able to form an answer to such an outrageous question. Please read on for further clarification.

A word about Gold Class cinema

Well, two words really. 'Don't' and 'bother'.

Some of my rules stand alone and need no explanation. Others I like to really hammer home and when it comes to Gold Class cinema, it's hammer time.

I am on a one-woman quest to change hearts and minds and convince everyone to abandon Gold Class cinema. My dream is that Gold Class sections will soon become empty wastelands and cinemas will be forced to return the space taken up by those ridiculously oversized seats to the regular movie-goer.

Gold Class is the dumbest thing ever and here's why:

The unique selling point of the Gold Class cinema 'experience' is the number one thing you don't need in a cinema —an elaborate food menu.

In Gold Class, you are offered everything from 'small plates' to 'larger plates' plus pizzas and ice-cream sundaes. From sweet potato fries and sliders to bruschetta and, my favourite menu item, salt and pepper squid. The obvious question to ask is, who is brave enough to order seafood at Hoyts? Some of those kids working behind the snack bar can barely shovel popcorn into a bucket—are you really going to trust those same kids to expertly prepare, then lightly flour and shallow fry, a delicate piece of seafood? Or are people under the misapprehension that the Gold Class cinema kitchen is where all the top chefs are working now?

*I don't understand the urge to combine two perfectly enjoyable separate activities, dinner **and** a movie, into dinner **during** a movie. What do we gain by combining them? Are we in a hurry? Do we not have time to do both things?*

You must also consider that most, if not all, of this food requires a knife and fork. Who wants to take on the challenge of eating a full meal with cutlery, in the dark, without looking down to see what they're doing lest they miss what's going on in the movie? Bear in mind, too, that where people are eating with knives and forks, there will be a lot of clanking and scraping, not to mention the Dolby Surround Sound 'smack-smacking' coming from punters sucking on buffalo wings with hot sauce.

Eating a full meal in the dark also pretty much guarantees you are going to walk out of 'Gold Class' looking decidedly 'Vagrant Class' with nachos dribble and ranch dressing spilled down your front and hot sauce smears all over your pants. Admit it, you're going to wipe your hands on your pants, 'cos it's dark and you won't be able to find your napkin.

Finally, let's not forget that all this food and beverage service requires waitstaff. An absurd addition to your movie-going experience. It's distracting enough in Plain Class cinema when fellow movie-goers get up and down in order to go to the toilet or replenish their trough of popcorn or top up their 44-gallon drum of soft drink. By employing waitstaff, Gold Class cinema is literally paying people to wander around the cinema and interrupt your movie viewing.

Just say no to Gold Class.

———————————————————————→

FOR MOVIE-MAKERS

This is a handy section for anyone writing or making a movie. If you think you have come up with something that seems a little unbelievable or not quite accurate, this quick checklist will help you.

285
Women wear shower caps when they shower

For a woman, washing and drying your hair can be a fairly time-consuming ordeal and not something you want to do every day. If a woman can get away without washing her hair, she will. Yet whenever women shower in the movies, they seem completely unconcerned about how long it is going to take to wash and dry their hair, and they almost always stick their entire head under the shower wetting down a perfectly good blowdry that would easily have lasted another day or two.

286
Women wash themselves to get clean not to get off

No woman runs her soapy hands all over herself in a languid, sensual way—she methodically scrubs her areas.

287
Women don't have pillow fights

Not even when they're at college and living in dorms with room-mates. Certainly no woman has ever had a pillow fight in her underwear. Pillow fights only happen in male movie directors' minds.

288
No one has sex on the kitchen floor

Why would you? Sure, the sexy times might start in the kitchen but people always move it to the bedroom. Not the kitchen bench. The bedroom is just down the hall, it has a comfortable bed in it. No matter how urgent you are, you can always call a thirty-second time-out to move proceedings to the bedroom.

289
Food fights don't happen in civilised households

There is no mother in the world who would tolerate a food fight. And certainly none that would encourage one. That scene where a child playfully throws a piece of spaghetti across the table, gets a shocked look from 'Mom' that soon spreads into a naughty, knowing smile from Mom as she reaches into her own plate of pasta and throws an even bigger handful of spaghetti across the table? You know that scene? Well, it's never happened.

290
Young children don't speak in snappy witty rejoinders

Not many adults do either. But pithy comebacks from kids and sage counsel from children wise beyond their years are particularly grating and unrealistic.

291
Don't let the actors spit

This is a rule for actors. Actors sometimes get so worked up and 'in the moment' that a bit of spit comes out during their dialogue. I'm not sure whether Daniel Day Lewis actually invented spit-acting but he certainly took it to a new level. The other serial offender/camel is Al Pacino. He likes to shout and he likes to spit, quite often all over his co-stars; and for an audience, that can be quite distracting.

Therefore, the rule for directors is, when there's too much spit flying around and especially when someone has a bit of spit yawing up and down in a string between their lips, please call cut and go again.

292
No hitting on younger women

This is a rule for both on screen and off. One of the main issues the #MeToo movement brought to the fore was that of older men hitting on younger women, with the men taking advantage of the power dynamic and the fact that they were the more senior members of the production. Now, I don't think older women necessarily enjoy being hit on by old men either; however, at least they are more likely to have the confidence and experience and, most importantly, the seniority to tell the old men to fuck off.

And perhaps if movies stopped casting much younger women to play the love interests of older men, then men would stop thinking that going out with much younger women is the norm. Don't get me wrong, I think young women are awesome—youth is undeniably seductive in its physical beauty—but speaking as an older woman with a lot of older women friends, my god we're an interesting bunch. I actually don't understand why older men don't want to get involved with women their own age. Seriously, we're pretty great. But then I guess I don't understand the urge to wank into a potplant either. So what do I know?

AT THE SHOPS

A word about Sunday trading

There used to be a corner shop in every neighbourhood that sold a bit of everything. Essential items like milk, bread, packets of French onion soup, and lollies for one cent a piece. When I think now about how long kids used to spend in front of the lolly counter directing the obliging shopkeep to give them 'one of those and two of those, one of the red things at the front . . . and um . . . how much are the snakes? Yep, okay one more of those . . .' all to make up a lolly bag worth the grand total of ten cents, it seems like shopkeepers back then were idiots—albeit incredibly patient and kind and generous idiots.

*In our area, the corner shop was referred to as 'The Robbers'. As in 'Hey, can someone pop down to The Robbers and get some milk?' So called because they charged ridiculously high prices, which they got away with because they stayed open late **and** they were open on Sundays. That used to be the holy grail, to find* a shop that was open on Sunday—it was the near-impossible dream. But now that dream has come true and it's come true in spades. What shop isn't open on Sunday? Shopping centres are the new church; these days when Sunday rolls around, the whole family heads off to worship at Westfield.

I realise it's extremely convenient to be able to do your shopping on a Sunday but I sometimes wonder whether it's a particularly fun way for children to spend the weekend—being dragged around a shopping centre to purchase some much-needed homewares, like an oversized vase full of sticks or some forty million thread count sheets or a milkshake maker (you need a special maker for milkshakes now—apparently blenders don't make milkshakes anymore).

But then again, it could be worse, I'd take standing around in Kmart while my mum decided if she needed a chocolate fountain any day over sitting in a pew listening to a priest bang on about a 2000-year-old street hustler who turned water into wine.

SHOP ASSISTANTS

293
Don't call anyone older than you 'darling'

Or 'darl' or 'babes' or 'sweetie' or 'hun', or any other bizarrely affectionate and over-familiar endearment. There is nothing more off-putting than walking into a shop and having a fresh-faced twenty-something greet you with, 'Can I help you, hun?'

By the way, this rule is moot for anyone from Northern England. Up there, referring to someone as 'pet' or 'love' is standard. They're born doing it and they couldn't stop doing it if they tried. It's in their DNA and it's neither sexist nor patronising, it crosses all ages and genders—everyone is called 'pet' or 'love'. Point is, it's charming coming from Carol in West Yorkshire, but not so much from Brianna in Westfield Chadstone.

294
Keep your banter vague

For some reason, everyone working in retail these days is desperate to know how your day is progressing. It's such a specific question: 'How's your day been so far?' I'm afraid, I don't have an answer to that question, especially at 9.30 in the morning when the day has barely begun. If you happen to be dealing with someone who genuinely wants to tell you how their day has been (like my friend Liz) then, trust me, they will volunteer that information without any prompting. She loves to give the sales assistant her life story, but she is a rare exception. With everyone else, you should just assume they are having an okay day—in fact, it was probably a pretty good day right up until you ruined it with your dumb question.

And further to this rule, never ever ask anyone over forty: 'Got any plans for the weekend?' We don't. The clue is in the item on the counter in front of you. I'm buying Cottontails and a comfortable beige bra, not the sort of thing worn by someone who goes clubbing, or attends music festivals or does anything else of interest on the weekend.

295
Acknowledge the customer standing at the counter

I will happily wait for you to finish whatever it is you are doing or pretending to do as long as you look up at me and say, 'I'll be with you in a minute.' And you don't even have to say it with your mouth, you can say it with your eyebrows and a small nod. On the whole, Australians are very patient people, provided we are acknowledged.

296
No hiding when you are supposed to be manning the register

I don't know where the register staff at Bondi Junction Myer disappear to every time I need to pay for something, but it's uncanny the way not a single person can be found at any register in any department once I am ready to make my purchase.

There have been several occasions when I have been forced to stand near the exit waving a prospective purchase through the sensors, setting off the alarms and shouting, 'I am going to steal this kettle if no one comes to serve me!'

297
Accept payment for goods at any and all registers

A good salesperson will find a way to take your money at whatever register you approach. It might mean opening a register specially for you or it might mean escorting you to the correct department and then jumping in behind that register. Either way, a decent sales assistant should just tappety-tap their staff number into the register and take your money. Because that's the job.

Some of the younger staff, however, tend to get rather separatist and refuse to allow cross pollination of departments, especially if it means doing some work, after all, it's much easier to fob a customer off and send them elsewhere. For example, I once had a young woman refuse to let me pay for a wooden spoon in the underwear section. She said I had to take it back to kitchenware and pay for it there. I wish I'd had the presence of mind to insist that the spoon *was* from the underwear department and that I'd found it in a bin marked 'special sex-spanking tools'. Just to see the look on her face.

ATTENTION, SUPERMARKET SHOPPERS

298
Don't get aggressive with the plastic shopping-demarcation divider

Some people get really testy when you start placing your items on the belt too close to theirs, and they will pick up that plastic divider thing and make a point of using it not only to mark the separation but also to push your items back a bit. There's really no need to panic, no one is trying to trick you into paying for their shopping and, I promise you, no one wants to steal your Birds Eye Potato Gems.

299
Once at the checkout, you are only allowed to run back for one item

If you've forgotten any more than one item, surrender your place in the queue and go and finish your shopping properly.

300
Don't be sucked in by this week's 'special buy' at Aldi

You don't need a log splitter, even at that unbeatable price.

301
Don't collect plastic rubbish at the checkout

Supermarkets can call these things 'collectables' but what they really mean is, 'useless bits of shit'. I can guarantee your limited edition set of miniature groceries will never appear on a future episode of *Antiques Roadshow*.

BIG SUPERMARKETS

302
Don't try to trick customers into buying your home brands

If your cheese is any good, I'll buy it. But don't insult my intelligence by packaging your Coles brand cheese to look like Mainland Tasty and then moving the Mainland Tasty right up high, out of my eyeline (and reach). You think I won't notice and will just buy your cheese instead without realising, but I won't. Because I'm quite stubborn and I have eyes. I'll either climb into the dairy cabinet and get the Mainland Tasty myself or I'll wait for someone tall to come along and ask them to get it for me. What I won't do is be tricked into buying your brand.

303
Program your self-service checkouts
to expect the obvious

For example, placing a bag in the bagging area should not be unexpected; it's the bagging area, it's for bags.

304
Don't complain about shoppers making mistakes

If you want to make sure avocados don't get put through as potatoes, go back to paying real people with eyes to work at your checkouts.

SPECIAL SEALED SECTION
CHANGE ROOMS

I have sealed this section because I assume it's of interest to ladies only. I know there are some men who are interested in change rooms but it's a very different kind of interest, one that I really can't get my head around. You read about these men every now and again in salacious news stories—they are the perverts who put hidden cameras in women's change rooms. And I have no idea why they do it, because I have rarely seen anything good looking back at me from the mirror in the women's change room.

Once, while attempting to squeeze into a too-tight swimsuit, I toppled over and head-butted the wall. The loud bang obviously alarmed the sales assistant, who immediately pulled back the curtain and asked, 'Is everything okay in there, sweetie?' Clearly everything was not okay, especially not now that I was on display to the entire shop. Everyone could see me leaning with my head 'resting' against the wall, unable to right myself due to the swimsuit trapped tightly around my thighs. Fortunately, I am a stickler for the rule of keeping one's underpants on while trying on swimmers so at least I wasn't busted with my bush out. However, that was of little consolation as I tried to fend off the young woman who had started to manhandle me

in a bid to stand me upright. She then unnecessarily offered
to bring me a larger size. I say unnecessarily because I had no
plans to stick around; as soon as my pants were back on, I was
hightailing it out of there. Hopefully that young sales assistant
will purchase a copy of this book and make a note of the most
important change-room rule:

305
No one but the person getting changed
is allowed to touch the curtain

This rule pertains mostly to sales assistants but also to mothers
who love to whisk that curtain back without warning so as to
expose the vulnerable half-naked changer within. These types
of people also have a warped sense of time; for them thirty
seconds feels like an eternity, which is why, less than a minute
after you've entered the change room, they are simultaneously
asking, 'How's it going in there?' and palming back the curtain.

306
The curtain must be bigger than the gap it is covering

It's unbelievable that this still needs to be said. It feels like women
have been complaining about fitting-room curtains that don't go
far enough across ever since fitting rooms and curtains were
invented. It's a very simple formula: you measure the gap then
order a curtain that is one and a half times that gap.

I've often wondered whether it was a women's clothing shop
owner who was responsible for ordering the rock they rolled in
front of Jesus's tomb. That would explain how the tomb came

to be empty three days later. JC obviously just slipped out the huge gap left on one side.

307
No mirror, no sale

I imagine it was a man who came up with the idea of not putting a mirror in the change room. The thinking behind this master stroke of psychology is that if a woman is forced to come back out into the shop in order to see herself in the mirror, the sales assistant can leap into action and start telling her how amayyyyzing she looks, thus increasing the likelihood of a sale.

There are two major flaws in this strategy. Firstly, it vastly underestimates a woman's intelligence. I'm not an idiot, I know when I look like a potato wearing a cardigan and no fast-talking sales assistant is going to convince me otherwise. Secondly, it fails to take into account the fact that there won't be any inter-action with any salesperson—because the minute I discover there are no mirrors in the change rooms, I'm turning around and walking straight out of the shop.

308
You're in a change room not an episode of *Cheers*

Everybody does not need to know your name. I am prepared to name and shame the store in question (it's Lululemon) because god knows they name and shame me every time I go in there. What is with all the questions, Lulu? Seriously, Lemon, why must you write my name on the change room door like I've been put on detention?

Also, I don't have an answer when one of your fit young things who works there starts quizzing me about what sort of exercise I do. Because I'm not looking for hot yoga pants or cold yoga pants or even tepid yoga pants. I don't need a 'tank' for Pilates or a bra top for jogging in. I'm just after some pants to wear when I walk my dogs and occasionally remember to tense my glute muscles for a few steps. Or, let's be completely honest, to sit around and watch television in while thinking about all the exercise I'm going to do ... starting tomorrow.

309
No men within a three-metre radius of the change rooms

Some women like to take their husband or boyfriend clothes shopping with them, which I find odd. I don't want to shop with any man I'm dating because I don't want to have explain why the white shirt I want to buy is different to the half a dozen other white shirts I already own. I want to buy what I like and not feel guilty about it.

But my main issue with it is that clothes shopping never looks fun for the man. He looks more like a hostage than a willing participant as he sits bored out of his scone in that chair that shops place outside the change rooms. The BHC I call it: the bored husband chair. And in a confluence of unfortunate factors, the shops that have the BHC also seem to have the DCG, the dreaded curtain gap. Now I'm not saying that someone else's bored husband would *want* to peer through that gap and look at me, I'm just saying he shouldn't have to. He's already suffering from extreme tedium, let's not punish him further with glimpses of things he will never be able to unsee. Do everyone a favour, ladies, and leave the partners at home.

TECHNOLOGY

A word about our own importance

At some point in recent history we all became really important, apparently, which is why we believe we must be contactable at all times. Where once you would leave the house and, by extension, the phone, because it was attached to the wall, now we take the phone everywhere, including places we don't really need it, like the movies, the gym, the park, the toilet, etc. All places where we are already engaged in an activity and shouldn't want to be interrupted.

I understand it's not just about being contactable. We rely on our phones for directions and also to make us look busy and important when we are alone in a cafe. I accept that the world has changed and that people aren't going to leave their phones at home. So my first rule for mobile phones is a compromise. I'm letting you have your phone, I'm just not letting you eat it too . . .

MOBILE PHONES

310
Don't answer your phone if you're busy

You are allowed to ignore your ringing phone. You don't have to drop everything to answer it. You can let the call go to voice-mail or simply make a note to call someone back later when you're not otherwise occupied. Remember, you're not obliged to prioritise the person on the other end of the phone who, for all intents and purposes, has just rudely interrupted by screaming, 'Pay attention to me!'

311
Use your inside voice

It's always preferable not to take a call if you are somewhere public, like on a bus or in a cafe or walking down the street. However, if you *must* take the call, use your inside voice and then turn it down even further. So let's say your outside voice is a ten; your inside voice should be a six and your mobile phone voice should be a four or a three. A lot of people get this rule arse-about and think their mobile phone voice should be an eleven. These people are ruining the world for everyone.

312
Don't walk and text

Pull over. Don't keep walking, and definitely don't stop dead in the flow of foot traffic and cause a Keystone Cop pile-up behind you. Stop and step to one side to do your texting.

313
No using speaker phone in public. Ever

Even worse than having to listen to someone talk on their mobile phone is being forced to endure *both* sides of the banal conversation because they are having it on speaker phone. More than being rude and inconsiderate, it is exceptionally arrogant to assume that your conversation is interesting enough to broadcast.

As for the youths who like to subject us all to their 'chunes' on public transport, it's a simple fact that your music would sound better through headphones. Honestly, I know nothing about speakers or woofers or subtweeters, but even I can hear that the tinny speaker on your iPhone is making your crappy taste in music sound even crappier.

314
Turn off the clackety texting noise

Texting should be a silent endeavour. No one should even know you're doing it. Young people, do us all a favour: take your parents' phones and turn off that infernal clacking sound for them.

315
Don't show anyone anything on a shattered screen

No one wants to look at a photo through a sad, fractured screen. You lose all showing privileges until you get that thing fixed.

316
No unauthorised swiping through someone's photos

When someone hands you their phone to look at a photo, you are supposed to look at the specific photo that is on the screen, comment appropriately, then hand the phone back. Don't take it upon yourself to browse through the rest of their photo library, swiping away left and right like you're on Tinder all of a sudden. You don't know what's on there—they could have all sorts of pics they don't want you to see. A note to my own friends and family: if you get to those photos of me and my cat in matching bonnets, you've definitely swiped too far.

317
Don't check your phone while someone is talking to you

Even if that person is really dull, it's extremely rude to pull out your phone and look at it while they are talking to you. Whether it's during dinner, while you're having a drink, or just chatting in the hallway at the office. Checking your phone is the equivalent of looking at your watch, yawning and walking off to talk to someone else mid-conversation. Don't do it.

318
Put your phone away when a friend is driving

Your friend is not your Uber driver or personal chauffeur. In giving you a lift, they are doing you a favour. Were they to use their phone during the ride, you'd probably end up wrapped around a telegraph pole, so extend them the same courtesy and stay off your phone while riding shotgun.

319
Don't be a phone-Mormon

Whether you choose Apple or Samsung or that brand the Chinese government can monitor (apparently), it's still just a phone. There's no need to evangelise about it in a bid to convert others. While it's entirely possible your phone is marginally better than the one your friend is using, the reality is no one is going to switch brands. So stop doing unpaid work for the phone companies. It's sad.

320
Never forget your mobile phone *is* mobile

This is a rule for people who like to take or make phone calls in the living room while others are present, usually watching TV. By all means, take or make your call, but do everyone a favour and move into another room to do it.

321
It's a phone, not a walkie-talkie

Don't be one of those people who holds the phone in front of their mouth and talks into it—just put it up to your ear. They've done the research, the results are in: holding it up to your ear and talking into it like a normal person won't kill you.

322
Don't leave a voicemail if it's important

This is actually just a private note for my friends and family. I never listen to my voicemails—if you need me to call you, just send a text.

EMAIL

323

Don't have an email address with more than one underscore

No one's writing that down. So unless it's the dummy email address you invented for giving to shop assistants (see next rule) pick a different permutation.

324

Invent a dummy email address
exclusively for shop assistants

We all have enough rubbish clogging our inboxes without being put on mailing lists by every shop we've ever spent a dollar in. So do what I do and just rattle off a pretend gmail account whenever a person behind a cash register asks for your details. And if there actually happens to be someone out there with the email address kittyunderscoreflanflanunderscore123@gmail.com, I sincerely apologise for all the retail junk mail you must be receiving courtesy of my excessive shopping habits.

325

Don't fire off emails that just simply say,
'Hey! Tell me all your news!'

Or any version of the above, such as *What's happening with you?!* or *Update me on your life!* That places the entire burden on the receiver to satisfy your random pang of neediness. It's up to you to contribute, to offer something of yourself that will in turn elicit a newsy response.

SOCIAL MEDIA

326
Don't use social media to communicate with your partner

Declaring feelings for your partner on social media has become quite the trend, even though it makes no sense whatsoever. Presumably, if they're your partner, you have their phone number, and there's a good chance you might even be living together—so next time you're overcome with feelings of love for them, why not send a quick text or, better yet, wait until they get home and tell them in person. Sending messages to a partner via social media is less about telling *them* something and more about telling the world how amazing *you* are. Look how nice you are sending appreciative, loving messages to your significant other. It's also a form of bragging, all that *so lucky to have this beautiful guy in my life, feeling pretty blessed right now hashtag sweetlove* is a not-so-subtle way of rubbing your happiness in everyone's faces. If you're really feeling so blessed, I suggest you call that beautiful guy direct 'cos I reckon he's a lot more interested in hearing about it than the rest of us.

327
Enjoy the event in real time not via Facebook posts

You're fooling no one with those good time party pics because if you were genuinely having a good time at the party, you'd be too busy having a good time at the party to be posting about having a good time at the party on Facebook.

328
Don't post pictures of yourself doing yoga

There is nothing more at odds with the philosophy of yoga than the world of Instagram. Yoga is supposed to be about self-reflection and inner peace and all that spiritual jazz. But how reflective and 'in the moment' can you really be when you're standing on a rock at sunset in your best Lululemons while your friend snaps off shot after shot of you warrior-posing it up with the waves crashing all around as you shout, 'Oh my god, hurry up, Felicia, we're losing the sun!'

Again, I would implore you to be original. If you must post pics of yourself exercising, why not entertain me with a quick little boomerang vid of you grapevining, 1980s Rancan Sisters-style.

329
Nobody wants to sign your change.org petition

I'm not disparaging your good intentions, I'm just suggesting there might be something more proactive you could do for a worthy cause that is clearly very close to your heart. Something that takes a little more effort than pressing the 'send to all my contacts' button.

330
Don't make a celebrity death all about you

When a celebrity dies, social media turns into the morbidity Olympics. Public mourning quickly becomes a competitive arms race to determine who is the saddest of them all. It's already a blow that the celebrity is dead but what's really depressing is that they aren't around to defend themselves and tell the world they weren't actually friends with @mattnobody on Twitter or Instagram.

331
A brag is a brag is a brag

The term 'humblebrag' was coined by Harris Wittels to call out the sort of faux humility people employ when they want to brag about themselves. For example, *I went out looking like a fat sweaty pig today and this cute guy still hit on me? How weird is that?* The only thing weird about it is that you just posted something that essentially says, *Holy shit, I am sooooo good looking!* Another example of a humblebrag is when a comedian or musician or actor posts something like: *How embarrassing, sitting in a cafe right now and there's a giant poster with my face on it in the window!* If it's that humiliating, you could always leave the cafe or not sit down there in the first place rather than tweet about it and draw everyone's attention to it.

Unfortunately, the word has now moved into the vernacular and people seem to think that by heading up their braggy post with the word 'humblebrag', it makes it okay. It doesn't. It's merely an admission that you know you're being a faux-humble narcissist. If you must brag, own it. Head your post with *Blatant brag about me*—we'll all respect you more.

332
Don't resort to hack expressions

Things like: *Love you to the moon and back, Feeling blessed, Hashtag gratitude.* We've all heard them a squizillion times. Make an effort, say something new that you thought of yourself like: 'Love you more than chip-on-a-stick.'

333
Use the term 'going viral' correctly

It means something has millions of views and has spread across newsfeeds exponentially in the manner of a virus. A lot of people tend to say, 'Oh my god, my post has gone viral!' when all their friends have liked something. But unless you're a Kardashian, it's doubtful you have enough friends to make your post go viral.

334
Dial down the 'please share' neediness

I like to make up my own mind about whether to share something or not, and I do that based on whether it is share-worthy, not because someone has implored me to 'please share this post!!' It's the same with reviews or podcasts that end by begging their listeners to 'please leave us a five star review'. If your podcast is any good I'll tell people about it, with my big mouth.

BLOGGING

Bloggers love to write 'from the heart' but sometimes they write from their arse by mistake. And unfortunately there is no curator of the internet; it's not like a newspaper or a magazine where there's an editor in charge of what gets published. Anything goes in Blogtown—it's like the Wild West, there are no rules and that's never a good thing. So think of me as the benevolent sheriff riding into town with all of my blogging rules to help make the World Wide Web a better place.

335
Don't presume people have hours to read your blog

Try to be concise. Much as you might like to write a stream of consciousness, people don't want to read it. Save your rambling innermost thoughts for your private diaries. When writing for public consumption, get to the point. Less waffle, more content. Limit your word count and think of it as writing an article instead of laying a blog.

336
Blogging won't make you rich

It just won't. No matter what people tell you about advertisers and people buying space on your hugely successful blog, it won't happen. So blog if you must, but do it because you enjoy it, not because you think you're going to make monster coin.

337
No topic, no blog

I realise this is difficult—believe me, I understand how hard it is to come up with a topic. In fact, I would go so far as to say that the hardest part of creating any content is coming up with the topic. I spent five years doing a segment on *The Project* every Tuesday and then another four years doing something similar on *The Weekly.* That's nine years of 'bits'. And for those nine years, the most torturous part of my week was not writing the jokes or filming the segment or remembering my lines in front of a live audience, it was coming up with the topic. But without a topic, you have nothing. Literally. However, many bloggers ignore this essential first step and just blog away. The thinking seems to be that if they admit they don't have a topic, then that absolves them, which is why you see a lot of blogs that start like this: *Hi guys, feeling pretty exhausted today, not really in the mood to blog but I know everyone's expecting a post from me so here goes . . .*

What usually follows is a meandering account of the blogger's day or week detailing why they feel bloated or tired (because they accidentally ate a pizza crust that wasn't gluten-free) or something about their painful haemorrhoids that are making it hard to sit down which is why they are standing up to write their blog today. In short, nothing anyone needs to hear about.

Remember, if you don't have a topic, don't blog. Make every post count.

338
Give me the recipe, not the story of your life

Recipe bloggers are notorious for using the recipe to lure you into reading about their lives. I have rarely clicked on a link to a recipe and been lucky enough to have that recipe magically appear on the page before me. Instead, what usually happens is that I am forced to scroll through pages of irrelevant inform- ation about how the blogger was feeling on the day they first made this recipe or how their kids and hubby 'love love love this dish!' There might be some arbitrary memories of their grand- mother, who always loved this time of year and would sweep the autumn leaves into giant piles for the children to kick about in. Oh the hours of fun to be had in Gram-gram's yard. Yeah, yeah, whatever, blogger, just give me the old lady's recipe for chocolate chip cookies.

339
Limit of one blog per person

If you must start a new blog, delete the old one. Blogs are like internet landfill—we are rapidly running out of room on the World Wide Web, so please dispose of your old blog thoughtfully before starting a new one.

INSTRUCTIONAL YOUTUBE VIDEOS

340
Get to the point. Quickly

When making an instructional YouTube video, you want to think of it as court testimony and present the facts, just the facts.

Because when someone is seeking information on something— whether it be how to re-grout a shower recess, or crochet a bobble stitch, or use Excel to make a spreadsheet—everyone wants the same thing: simple, clear, step-by-step instructions. And that's it. No one is interested in tinkly music and fun graphics, and trust me when I say that absolutely no one wants to sit through a two-minute introduction where the 'Tuber' waves hello and tells the viewer all about themselves and then explains what the video is going to be about.

These 'film-makers' have no idea how boring their presentations are because they don't have the benefit of a live audience. They just make the video, upload it and that's it. They don't get to see the reaction of the viewer watching the video. So, for the YouTuber's edification and in a bid to improve the standard of YouTube clips across the board, I have transcribed a video I tried to watch recently and inserted the viewer's thoughts throughout.

YOUTUBER: 'Hi, I'm Carly, I'm a stay at home mom and I lerve doing a bit of DIY around the house . . .'

VIEWER: *Good for you, Carly, not at all relevant, please move on.*

YOUTUBER: 'Today I'm going to show you how to re-grout your shower recess.'

VIEWER: *Yep, I know that already 'cos I googled 'how to re-grout your shower recess' so get on with it.*

YOUTUBER: 'Regrouting your shower is an easy way to give your bathroom a complete lift.'

VIEWER: *Oh my god, I know! That's why I want to do it, come on already.*

YOUTUBER: 'When I moved into this apartment the shower recess looked like this . . . not great, huh?'

VIEWER: *Don't care, your voice is annoying and I hate your hairdo, I'm starting to see why people leave abusive comments on YouTube, this is really irritating.*

YOUTUBER: 'But now, thanks to a bit of hard work from me and my boyfriend, it looks like this . . .'

VIEWER: *Okay, forget it, I'm done. We're 49 seconds in, there's been no useful information, I'm clicking elsewhere. I came for instructions on grouting, Carly, not to be your gal pal. Also, how in god's name do you have a boyfriend when you are this boring? And no, I'm not going to leave you a five star review, I have a rule about that sort of thing.*

INTERNET COMMENTING

341
Don't read the comments section

You'll only work yourself into a bate, and possibly even be tempted to break the following rule.

342
Don't write in the comments section

It's like shouting into the air. Pointless and a sign of madness.

343
If you *must* write in the comments section, leave your full name

If you're not prepared to leave your full name and own your opinion, you don't get to share your opinion.

344
If you must write in the comments section *about me*, leave your full name *and* phone number

Because I would like to talk to you personally, mostly about your spelling and grammar. Helpful little things, like:

- YOU'RE is a contraction of 'you are', as in 'you are an idiot'.
- YOUR is a possessive pronoun, as in 'if you can't spell, that's <u>your</u> problem'.

We may also need to discuss the difference between 'bought' and 'brought'. And that you lend money *to* someone and you borrow money *from* someone but you never lend money *off* someone. Oh, and paedophile has an 'a' in it.

345
If the humour article is not making you laugh, stop reading it

Comedy is subjective and we all find different things funny. Some people don't find anything funny. The good news is, there is actually a fair bit of content on the internet, so if you're not enjoying something, you can click on something else. No need to punish yourself by reading the whole thing, working yourself into an apoplectic state and then shouting all over the comments section: 'THIS ARTICLE IS NOT FUNNY!!' or 'WHAT A STUPID WASTE OF TIME THIS ARTICLE IS!'

Shhhh, it's okay, close the article and either go watch a cat video, or maybe take some crack to calm down.

346
Fact trumps opinion

When presented with facts based on proven, peer-reviewed science, the phrase 'Well, that's just your opinion' is not a valid argument. It's like being told: 'According to the Bureau of Meteorology, yesterday it was 27 degrees outside' and you saying, 'Well, that's just your opinion.' No, no, that's a fact.

347
You must read the whole article before commenting

You cannot just look at the headline or the photograph attached to the article, draw your own spurious conclusions and then spew out a comment. You are required to read the entire piece and make sure you understand not only the context but also the fact that the headline or photo may well have been ironic. Then you can comment. If you must.

348
Make your comment relevant to the post

Some people like to use the comments box to tell stories about themselves. They lure you in with one quick remark about the post and then segue very unsubtly into a story about their life. For example:

> Hey, great article about brownies. I am currently in talks with a publisher about my memoir. It's about my childhood in Ireland. I was beaten by nuns, shared one pair of shoes with my three sisters, and my mother never made us brownies. Sadly, she was always too busy working. We discovered years later, she was the village prostitute, we always thought she just had lots of boyfriends. Because she worked from home, we got sent to the library a lot. And that's how I fell in love with books. Books were my escape and now it looks like I will get one published. Yay! Thanks for posting.

349
Don't engage with comment terrorists

These are people who like to hijack the comments and steer them off into uncharted and completely irrelevant territory. Essentially they are looking to provoke a fight with a stranger. For example, in a news item about a missing woman, the hijacker will seize control of the comments box by writing something like:

She looks like a botox whore!

To which someone else will reply:

Shutup I know her, shes my friend and she so isn't a botox whore, why don't you go back to where you came from.

And then the hijacker is straight back in with:

I'm from here u dumb slut, I guess U must be a botox whore to.

As you can see, it's now just a good, solid debate about a missing woman who may or may not have had Botox and who some people think might be a sex worker, even though the news item never mentioned either of those things. Don't let the comment terrorists win.

SPORT

A word about sport

I am not enough of a sports enthusiast to pull off a convincing list of sporting rules—but I also don't believe in trashing something so important to a large percentage of the population. The exception, of course, is Rugby League, specifically the NRL and the lady-hatin' culture that they just can't seem to eradicate.

So, apart from my one raging blind spot with regards to Rugby League, I am not actually a sport-hater nor am I completely ignorant about sport. In fact, in the eighties I was quite the cricket fan. But who wasn't back then? The West Indies reigned supreme and Viv Richards et al. showed us that cricketers didn't have to look like pie-munching, beer-bellied, seventies porn stars. On the contrary, they looked like athletic gods and everyone loved them, even when they came out here and beat Australia.

However, the thing I remember most about going to the cricket during that era was that there was no booing. People may have booed a display of bad sportsmanship, such as underarm bowling or 'chucking', but there was no booing the rival team for playing well and winning. You didn't boo because your team was losing, and you certainly didn't heckle and harass individual players from the stands.

Booing seems to have become accepted behaviour these days, with fans very quick to get all Joaquin Phoenixy from Gladiator, jeering and thumbs-downing the players they don't like. If I wanted to be trite, I'd say something like 'and I think that really sums up everything that's wrong with the world today'. But let's not be clichéd and platitudinous about things, after all, I'm not a sportsperson giving a post-game interview.

For this section, I wanted to be fair and impartial and acknow-ledge that society is made up of two different types of people, those who are really into sport and those who aren't. Thus I have provided rules for both sides.

———————————————→

FOR SPORTS FANS

350
No booing

Save your booing for the baddy that's 'behind you' in a panto-mime. But don't boo elite sportspeople for doing their job well.

351
You have Friday and Monday to talk about the weekend's game

That's it. One day of pre-game chatter and one day of post-game chatter, then let it go.

352
Keep your obscure stats to yourself

You might be the Rainman of football and know everything there is to know about every game ever played, but when you dominate the space with that kind of forensic knowledge you completely alienate the lesser sports fans who are trying to join in. The way to bring a cross-section of people into the conversation is to casually drop a titbit of salacious sports-related gossip. Everyone can get on board talking about the WAG who got busted for shoplifting or the player who tested positive for cocaine and Optifast shakes. No one, however, knows who you're talking about when you refer-ence some legendary mark taken in a VFL game back in 1927, even if it was 'a classic'.

353
No mocking the person coming last in the office tipping competition

Just appreciate that Jenny from Accounts is joining in.

354
Don't take a loss so seriously that it affects your mood for the rest of the day/week/month

Remember, it's just a game, nobody died.

FOR NON-ENTHUSIASTS

355
Never tell a fan: 'It's just a game, nobody died'

Let someone be sad if their team loses.

356
Don't reject the entire notion of sport out of hand

There is nothing to be gained from loudly lamenting the fact that sport gets more funding than theatre. Sport is massively popular for a reason and that's because it's actually quite accessible. If you give it ten minutes, you can usually work out the rules for most games, which is more than can be said for Shakespeare or Beckett or John—*Paradise Lost*—Milton. (Does anyone know what the f*%k that book is about?)

357
You can't suddenly become a fan just because a team starts winning

Nobody likes a Jenny-from-Accounts-come-lately.

358
Don't say dumb stuff to derail a conversation about sport

Not every conversation has to be about you—accept that some people enjoy talking about sport and don't try to pull focus by feigning over-the-top ignorance: 'Who's this guy Carlton? What? It's a team? Never heard of them. What are we talking about here? Baseball? Lacrosse? Rounders? Sorry, everyone, but I don't follow the *Sportsball*.'

Even if you genuinely don't know who or what Carlton is, you can probably figure it out by listening for context-based clues. So, don't be a dick, try harder.

359
Avoid jokes about soccer being a boring, low-scoring game where nothing happens

It's true but it's a bit hack to make those kinds of jokes. I feel bad for including one here.

360
Don't pretend to like a team just because the guy you like likes them

Ladies, you know who you are and this kind of behaviour demeans us all.

SPECIAL RULES FOR FOOTBALLERS

361
Never assume a woman wants to have sex with you

Always ask the woman whether she wants to have sex with you.
I know, it seems so obvious and yet . . .

362
Embrace the urge to get nude and
sexual with your team-mates

What I'm suggesting is, why not leave the woman out of it?
I'm talking about those cases where multiple footballers are
alleged to have had group sex with one woman or when some of
the team has hidden in a cupboard and watched on while others
have had sex with a woman. To me, it seems like sometimes the
woman is only there to give the whole thing a thin veneer of
heterosexuality and that you would probably all be quite happy
just doing each other, and who can blame you? You're all elite-
level athletes, you're all in great shape, you're all passionate about
your footy and you love each other as mates. Why wouldn't you
want to get physical with one another? In fact, it might even
improve your performance as a team. It worked for the Spartans.
Some historians believe it was actually all the man-love going on
in that army that made them such a formidable fighting force.

After all, it's just sex, right—it doesn't mean anything (well,
that certainly seems to be the attitude when there's a woman
involved).

363
Never assume a woman wants to have sex with you

Oh hang on, I said this one already. You know what, I think it bears repeating. Always ask the woman whether she wants to have sex with you. And then maybe ask again just to make sure you heard her right.

PARTIES & CELEBRATIONS

A word about parties

I have never had a party. I've been to parties but I've never had a party, not even a twenty-first. I had a 'morning tea' instead. As a kid, my mother would give me the choice every year, 'Do you want a birthday party or would you rather go out for dinner with the family?' I chose dinner with the family every time. And yes, it was mostly because I loved dining at upmarket restaur-ants (like the Pizza Hut), but I think there was also a nagging fear that I might have a party and no one would turn up. I've often wondered if that's where the whole routine of inviting the entire class stemmed from —perhaps it's nothing to do with not wanting to leave anyone out, and more about kids hedging their bets and making sure they get a decent turnout.

INVITATIONS AND ATTENDANCE

364
Late notice cancellations can't be texted

If you want to cancel on the day of the event, you have to suck it up, make an actual phone call and explain yourself. When you text through a last-minute cancellation, you revoke your right to be believed. Texted excuses are malarkey, everyone knows that.

365
Verbal invitations must contain specifics

It's quite common (and ill mannered, according to my mother) to pose an invitation as a vague question. Something like:

'Hey! What are you doing Friday night?'

This puts the invitee in a real pickle. Do they admit to being free or not? What if you're about to invite them somewhere really great? They don't want to say 'I'm busy' and risk missing out. On the other hand, what if it's an invitation to the Hog's Breath Cafe where you'll get to watch Pam from Sales get wasted on dollar drinks while Brian from IT eats a steak bigger than his head.

The correct way to invite someone to something is to spell out all the details in your initial pitch, thereby leaving the invitee room to lie if they'd rather be dead than attend. For example:

'Hey! A bunch of us are going out for dinner on Friday night, Pam from Sales, Julia from Accounts, Sue from HR, the whole gang from IT, we're going to the Hog's Breath Cafe. It's half-price cocktails between six and seven. Want to come?'

The person now knows everything they need to, and can confidently answer:

'Oh gosh, I'm sorry, I can't, I'm busy on Friday . . . I have . . . something on. Bummer.'

Always state your business up front and allow people plenty of room to invent an excuse if need be.

366
You don't have to farewell the entire room

Just say goodbye to the host and anyone else you happen to pass on your way out. You absolutely do not have to go around the entire party and farewell everyone you know. It should take you five minutes maximum to leave a party, not forty-five.

367
When cycling to events, take a few moments outside to recover before making your entrance

No one wants to kiss your sweaty cheek or shake your clammy hand.

BIRTHDAYS

368
A birthday text is sufficient

Let's be honest, no one really wants a birthday call. Let alone a string of them throughout the day. Except your mum. She's the exception—always call your mother on her birthday.

369
Facebook birthday greetings are insincere and meaningless

Everyone knows the reminder came up automatically on your Facebook feed and that you didn't actually remember yourself. By sending a Facebook message, you are simply acknowledging the fact that you forgot your friend's birthday. It's great to get that little reminder but what you should do is remove Facebook from the equation and compose a birthday text message instead. That way you give the impression that it was you, not Mark Zuckerberg, who actually remembered this special day.

370
Don't mix your friends—have multiple birthday events instead

Intermingling of friends is hard work. And the onus to do all that work invariably falls on you as the single common denominator between people. So save yourself the trouble and schedule several birthday events instead.

DINNER PARTIES

371
If someone brings fancy wine to your dinner party, you must open it

Don't be one of those people (we all know them) who looks at the nice wine or Champagne they are handed on arrival and says, 'Ooh, lovely!' and then puts it in a cupboard, clearly indicating they have no intention of opening it. White wine goes in the fridge; red wine stays on the kitchen bench—both these actions signal the 'intent to serve'. If it's a particularly special bottle and you don't happen to get around to serving it, the classy thing to do is keep it aside and bring it out the next time that person visits.

372
If you tell guests not to bring anything, don't be annoyed when they don't bring anything

373
If your host tells you not to bring anything, be sure to bring something

374
An intolerance is not an allergy

If you are allergic to shellfish or nuts or mutton chops, by all means inform your host because no one wants a dead dinner guest at the table, that's a real downer. Likewise, if you're going to swell up and turn purple, Violet Beauregarde-style, or break out in hives, then please make that information known ahead of time. But if you're calling your host to tell her that you're trying to 'avoid carbs at the moment' then maybe it's better to just turn down invitations to dinner parties altogether.

375
Don't ostracise the vegan

I respect, nay, I applaud the lifestyle choice of the vegan. Vegans are only trying to make the planet a better place for everyone, so we must not mock and deride their decisions.

376
Vegans must lower their expectations

In return for my respecting a vegan's beliefs, I ask that the vegan respect my limited culinary abilities. For even though I am a decent cook, I do not have the skills or knowledge to make tasty vegan food. Vegetarian dishes I can whip up no problem, but if you take away my cheese and my yoghurt and my honey and my eggs and basically every other ingredient in my fridge and pantry, then I'm afraid all I can offer you is a big bowl of air. My point is, I am happy to dine with vegans, I am happy to eat vegan food; however, you can't expect me to cook that food for you. The onus is on the vegan to source a restaurant with vegan options or invite me over for some tasteless chaff and beans. I promise I will smile politely and say, 'Mmm, that's delicious, I think I can actually taste the planet being saved!'

377
Put some music on

Actually this is not so much a rule as another one of my notes to self. I am notorious for hosting dinner parties and forgetting to create a bit of ambience. The thing is, I actually enjoy cooking in a nice quiet kitchen. Which is fine, provided I remember to put some music on when the guests arrive. No one wants to eat dinner accompanied only by the sounds of knives and forks scraping across plates and my recounting, in great detail, the latest series I watched on Netflix.

378
No hiving

'Hiving' is when you separate or 'hive' someone off from the group and monopolise them. Couples who have been together a long time (like my parents) are notorious for this behaviour. It occurs when one of the couple (usually my dad) is telling a story that the other one (usually my mum) has already heard and so to avoid having to sit through the story for the umpteenth time, the other one (my mum) 'hives off' the person sitting next to her and starts up a separate and often intense one-on-one exchange. Hivers are the conversational equivalent of a defensive player in netball or basketball who body-blocks their opponent and prevents them from getting involved in the normal run of play.

379
No more than six people at a dinner party

Sometimes you can't avoid big numbers, like at Christmas lunch or a family birthday, but when you are simply having a few people over for dinner, you should cap your guest list at six. Cooking for six is manageable. You'll have enough plates, you'll have enough serving dishes and you shouldn't need to buy catering-size quantities of any ingredient.

More importantly, six is the magic number for dinner table conversation. Once you go over six guests, you end up with at least two conversations happening at the table and usually one of those conversations is far more interesting than the other. Invariably you will get stuck just out of range of *that* conversation and, what's worse, you could find yourself 'hived off' by the really earnest guy who's married to your friend even though you've never known what she sees in him.

Meanwhile, you keep catching juicy snippets of the conversation happening at the other end of the table, involving someone who worked on a reality TV show or whose cousin went to school with Nicole Kidman and who, 'swear to god', actually saw the ten-year marriage contract she had with Tom Cruise. At least that's what you think they're saying, it's hard to hear anything over the drone of the hiver.

380
Read the room, know when the party is over

Once the host has stopped opening wine and has moved on to serving hot beverages, chances are the party is winding down, so be on the lookout for further clues, such as the host yawning or leaving the table to start doing the dishes. If the conversation is cracking along and everyone's still having a great time, the only reason the host will leave the table is to open another bottle of wine.

And if the host goes to bed, party's over, get out.

WEDDINGS

381
One wedding is plenty

I don't care how many times you get married but you are only allowed one Billy Idol-style 'white wedding', the type that comes with all that solemn gazing into one another's eyes vowing to take each other 'in sickness and in health' and 'till death do you part' business. When you've made such a grand to-do of promising to stay with someone until they're dead and then just a few years later, decide there's no way you can wait for this clown to die and you want a divorce, then you give up your right to make those sorts of melodramatic promises ever again. Because you clearly don't mean it. By all means, get married again and have a gathering to celebrate your union, but don't make everyone sit through another whole churchy wedding and earnest public declaration of your intent to see one another to the grave. And no more gifts. Enough with the gifts.

382
It's a wedding not a GoFundMe campaign

If you say 'Your presence is our present'—mean it. There should not be a hyperlink included on the invitation where guests can click and 'donate now' to your honeymoon fund.

383
Don't be offended if you are not chosen to be bridesmaid

Rejoice.

384
Get an honest friend to review your 'self-penned' vows before the wedding

Writing your own vows is a difficult thing to do well. There's a reason those stock-standard vows became stock standards. The best self-written vow I've ever heard was from a woman who asked her partner to promise he would always swap meals with her if they were out at a restaurant and she was suffering from order-envy. He vowed that he would. I bet *they're* together till they die because that is a really good vow.

385
No gift registries

Most couples these days have been living out of home for quite some time and already have a lot of stuff, so the wedding registry is really just two people wandering around a department store with a price scanner pointing and clicking at things they want but don't need. It's the equivalent of a child sitting on Santa's lap with an outrageous twenty-page list of demands for Christmas.

Getting married should not be viewed as an opportunity to refurbish your house with expensive items. If you can't afford to buy those things yourself, you shouldn't expect your friends to buy them for you either. If you *can* afford to buy them for yourself, then you should buy them for yourself.

To be clear, I'm not saying no gifts. I'm happy to buy you a gift, I just don't want to be handed a set of instructions on how to do it or how much you'd like me to spend.

I am well aware that hardly anyone else shares this view, which is why I have set up a special hotline. If you feel the need to vent your opinion about *my* opinion on gift registries, simply call *1800 FUCK YOU FLANAGAN I LIKE STUFF.*

386
Don't call it a wedding invite

It's an invitation. You invite people to your wedding with an invitation.

387
Be specific with your dress code

You can set any dress code you like for your wedding, just make sure you explain it fully. The more detail the better. After all, most people, especially the ones reading this book, appreciate rules. And don't be afraid to use your wedding to enforce your personal moral codes on others, no matter how at odds they might be with current societal attitudes. Your day, your rules. For example, my wedding dress code would read: *You may wear a short skirt OR a low-cut top; you may not, however, wear both —let's keep it classy, ladies.*

388
One venue. No shuttle buses

Your friends will enjoy your wedding so much more if they don't have to move venues. Try to have the wedding and reception in the same place. I don't care how great the second venue is, if I have to get on a shuttle bus to get there then I'd rather stay put and eat pikelets at a trestle table in the church car park. After a few drinks, no one will care where they are anyway, so why not have everything all in one spot.

389
Treat your bridesmaids like grown-ups and don't put them in matching frocks

If you must follow 'tradition' and have your bridesmaids in matching dresses, then do it properly. The custom hails back to Roman times when bridesmaids wore the exact same dress *as the bride*. It was done to create a bunch of decoys on the altar that would ward off evil spirits as well as confuse any angry, rejected suitors who might turn up wanting to harm the bride. So if you're not prepared to have all your gal pals in exactly the same fancy white dress as yours, then respect the fact that they all have different body shapes and different complexions and don't put everyone in the same strapless fuchsia bandage dress. You're not trying to recreate Robert Palmer's 'Addicted to Love' video.

390
All you need is one good wedding photo

And that is a photo where you both look like decent versions of yourselves, where you both look happy to be there and neither of you have hair blowing across your face. Once you have that, relax, stand down the photographer, and head to the reception to be with your guests and enjoy your wedding.

The tediously long photo shoot with multiple locations is a construct invented by the wedding photographer to justify charging you an obscene amount of money. In this digital age when you can see the photos immediately and ascertain whether you have a good one, there is no longer any need to snap off hundreds of 'just in case' photos. And there's certainly no need for a variety of backgrounds. Take the photos at the actual wedding venue and that way you'll remember the moment. You won't look back at photos in thirty years and say, 'Hmm, I don't remember getting married on a cliff . . . or in a forest . . . or near a lake . . . or by the beach. Also . . . why are we jumping in the air? Was there a rat? Did the Best Man goose me?'

391
No one is fooled by the 'candid' snap of a groom putting on cufflinks

All this photo says is 'the photographer told me to look pensive and fiddle with my cufflinks'.

392
The bride should remain vertical in all photos

Say no to any requests for a photo of the bride being held horizontal by all of the groomsmen. She's not a showgirl.

SPECIAL SEALED SECTION
WEDDING SPEECHES

I have sealed this section because I understand some people think there is no need for rules about wedding speeches. In fact, they believe the most entertaining part of a wedding is speech time, and by laying down a bunch of rules I am potentially ruining their opportunity to witness a classic train-wreck speech. And I understand your concerns but I don't think you need to worry. I once attended a wedding where the groom stood up and sang 'Wind Beneath My Wings' acapella to his 'beautiful lady' and no rule would ever have stopped him. He had a plan, he had a dream and he was determined to see it through. Hats off to him. He sang from the heart and it was one of the most memorable things I have ever seen. It was excruciating but I wouldn't change it for the world. My point is, I'm quite happy for you to take or leave this next section of rules, it's just here for anyone who would like a bit of help in avoiding being entertaining for the wrong reasons.

393
Five minutes, be funny, and get off

These were the inspiring words imparted to me by my mother as I stood up to make a speech at my sister's wedding. It was sound advice.

She also tapped her watch impatiently at me around the four-minute mark during my speech just in case I'd forgotten her instruction to 'keep it tight'.

It's a good idea to appoint a timekeeper for speeches— someone at the official table like a bridesmaid. She can ring a little bell when the speaker has one minute left. Because a good speech very quickly becomes a bad speech once it turns into a long speech.

394
Be relevant

It's not a twenty-first so forgo any hilarious stories about the bride or groom getting trashed and throwing up in a bin when they were fourteen. And it's not a lifetime achievement award either, no one is interested in a speech that chronicles every one of the bride's qualifications and accomplishments. Fathers tend to give this kind of LinkedIn profile speech when they think their daughter is too good for the man they are marrying. It's a passive-aggressive and public way of pointing up the disparity between the young lovers.

Finally, any anecdotes should be relevant in some way to the couple and/or their coupling, not just one of the individuals.

395
If you can't be funny, be sincere

I'm not suggesting you sing an acapella version of 'Wind Beneath My Wings' but no one will judge you if you speak from the heart, especially if you keep it brief.

396
Sex plus time does not equal comedy

This advice is specifically for The Best Man.

It's best not to bring up any incident that involves the bride doing anything or anyone, no matter how long ago it might have been or how many years it was before she met the groom. It's still not funny—especially when her parents and grandparents are in the room. Likewise, ditch any references to the groom 'banging' his way around Europe or to his lonely wanking days finally being over. Even if these tales killed at the bucks party, they will never be funny at the wedding. Not for the right reasons anyway. If in doubt, leave out any story that features or references a penis in any way.

397
Lay off the booze until after you've given your speech

The more you drink, the funnier you think you are and that's never a good thing when you're talking in front of an audience. It's always far better if the audience has had more to drink than you. So use your time wisely before the speeches: circulate and top up people's glasses.

398
Never start an anecdote with 'Here's a funny story . . .'

This is a general rule for life, not only for wedding speeches. Better not to raise people's expectations unnecessarily. Just tell your story and let the audience decide for themselves whether it's funny or not.

399
Cap the number of speeches

No need to hear from everyone, it's not a royal commission.

HALLOWEEN

400
Resisting Halloween is futile

Stop getting angry and faux-nationalistic about it. It's too late to try to reject Halloween as an American tradition that has no place here; we must accept that it's taken hold and realise it was always going to be a tough one to fend off. Why wouldn't kids want to celebrate Halloween? They get to dress up and they get free lollies. Kids don't care where the tradition comes from if there are costumes and free lollies involved.

401
Don't call it candy

Embracing an American tradition is one thing but let's maintain our own language standards.

402
Witches are scary not sexy

No one minds when parents join in on the dressing up, provided they dress up as something befitting the scary Halloween theme. However, what is fast becoming the norm among the yummier of mummies is the sexy witch 'costume'—which is really just mummy in a short black dress, a pointy hat set at a jaunty angle and a pair of too-high heels. Apart from there being no such thing as a sexy witch, Halloween is all about walking. You walk around the neighbourhood knocking on doors asking for free lollies. So wear appropriate footwear for such an event and remember you're out trawling for sugar for your kids not a sugar daddy for yourself.

403
Tell your kids to say thank you

One year I decided not to be the neighbourhood grouch and to actually get involved with Halloween. I stuck foam skulls on the fence spikes outside my house to indicate 'sugar-seeking children welcome here' and bought a whole load of Furry Friends—which, if you don't know, are flat thin bars of milk chocolate with an Australian animal on the wrapper. (I was joining in but I still wanted to make a cultural statement.)

The first Trick or Treaters arrived at around 4.30 pm, I opened the door, commented on their outfits (which weren't great but I still pretended to be impressed) and offered them the bowl of Furry Friends. One child took a bar with a kookaburra on it, said nothing and put it in her sugar sack; the other child took one, examined it then looked up at me and said, 'What is it?' I told her, 'It's a Furry Friend, it's chocolate, with a numbat on the wrapper ... yummy!' She wordlessly dropped it back into the bowl and returned empty-handed to her mother, who was waiting out on the footpath. There, they had a quiet, mumbled exchange, which appeared to end in the mother *consoling* the child before heading off to the next house. At no point did anyone call out 'thank you'. Not even the mother, she just shot me a withering look, as if to say, 'Children don't like Furry Friends, you idiot. I hope you're pleased with yourself because you have just ruined Halloween!'

Point taken. Next time I'll be like my own mother who drops unwrapped Scotch Finger biscuits into kids' treat bags. Kids certainly learned to avoid her house pretty quickly.

XMAS, NEW YEAR'S EVE AND THE OTHER ONE

404
Don't get a photo taken with Santa unless you're a child

The spontaneous 'Hey! Let's get a photo with Santa' idea is only funny for you and your friend. No one else thinks it's cute or hilarious. Plus it's about thirty bucks. And you have to wait in a queue. Go have coffee and cake instead.

405
Fireworks displays should be three minutes maximum

After fireworks have been banging in the sky for a few minutes you can really only see smoke anyway. And by the three-minute mark we've pretty much seen all the colour and shape combinations, it's now just variations on a theme and it stopped being in time with the simulcast soundtrack two minutes ago.

406
Enough with the exploding Harbour Bridge

This rule is for the NSW government: why don't you surprise the world one year by *not* firing a billion dollars' worth of fireworks off the Harbour Bridge?

407
Flags are not capes

That's a rule for every day by the way, not just Australia Day.

HOLIDAYS & TRAVEL

AUSTRALIANS OVERSEAS

408
Never say you want to 'do' a country

Say 'I would like to go to Cuba' rather than 'I really want to do Cuba'. Doing a country sounds obnoxious and unnecessarily sexual.

409
Holiday attire is only for the holiday

For some reason, you can get away with a different look when you are away from home. But trust me, that Bintang singlet and man-beads you wore for ten days in Bali or the acres of floaty linen and gold-roped espadrilles you wore in Noosa really won't pass muster back home.

410
Dress appropriately for the country you are visiting

For example, a football jersey is not appropriate attire for visiting the Vatican. Singlets and thongs may be appropriate in Thailand or Bali but if you are visiting a European capital city, probably best not to wear one of those weird tank tops with the giant armholes that show off your man nips. If in doubt, take your cue from the locals. Do the Parisian men have their man nips on display? No? Then put yours away.

411
Haggling is not compulsory

Before you dig your heels in and start trying to screw that local down in order to get yourself a bargain, do some maths and convert the price to Australian dollars. Then ask yourself, do you really need to save another six cents on a scrap of tie-dyed fabric that you plan to (but never will) turn into a cushion cover when you get home?

If you really must barter, then at least have the decency not to defend your quibbling by telling everyone, 'Oh but they expect you to haggle.' I promise you no stallholder ever went home from a long day at the market with a bit of extra cash in his pocket bemoaning the fact that he was insulted by fleshy white people who paid full price and refused to honour the local culture by haggling.

412
You are not King Kong, you don't have to climb on or up everything

Sometimes it's nice to just look *at* things like the Eiffel Tower or the Harbour Bridge or Uluru or the Empire State Building rather than stand atop them. You are no less of a traveller because you didn't physically mount the landmark.

A word about bunking in

There is staying with friends (or relatives) and then there is 'bunking in'. It becomes bunking in the minute you have to get creative with sleeping arrangements, i.e. when there are more houseguests than there are bedrooms to accommodate them. Young people are excellent at bunking in because for them it's all about priorities. They will happily sleep in a bathtub if it means they have a few extra bucks to spend on something more important, like beer. I find country people are often very relaxed about bunking in too, they have a generous, 'the more the merrier' attitude towards it. I wish I could be like that, but unfortunately I'm a dyed-in-the-wool city mouse who'd rather sell her own grandmother to get cash for a hotel room than sleep on someone's floor and share one toilet between ten people.

I have done my share of bunking in, most of it during a relationship I had with a guy whose entire extended family loved a
bunk-in. It was actually their preferred style of accommodations,
everyone all in together, sleeping wherever you can and not caring
that unless you're up and into the bathroom before dawn, you
won't be getting a hot shower. Each Christmas, my partner and
his kids, plus his two sisters, their partners and their kids would
set off from different parts of the country and trek to the Gold
Coast for the annual bunk-in at Mum's place. For two weeks. A
modest, three-bedroom, one-bathroom bungalow housed seven
adults, five children and three 'youths'. 'Youths' is the term I use
for male teenagers and it's important to note that youths take
up more space than either children or adults, not just with their
physical size but with their excess energy. Youths can't sit still,
they fidget, they knee tremble, they bounce balls, they relentlessly click and unclick pens—and don't leave chopsticks within
their reach or they'll be drumming on every available surface,
including toddlers and pets.

Up at Mum's on 'The Goldie', the kids slept wherever there
was space; on lilos and thin bits of foam, top to toe on the couch
and the day bed. I guess that's the beauty of kids; they go hard
all day and then they quite literally pass out as soon as they lie
down, wherever that might be.

After participating in one of these bunk-ins, I decided that
was enough and the next year I rented a nearby Airbnb. It had
four bedrooms and two bathrooms and I was happy to share
it. So long as I got the master bedroom with the en suite, the
rest was up for grabs—even the youths were welcome to join
us. I assumed I would be hailed a hero; I mean this was such a

good idea, it gave us more beds, more bathrooms, more kitchen space and, most importantly, more fridge space, because during a bunk-in, even a fridge cranked up to maximum struggles to keep anything above room temperature due to how often it is being opened and closed.

Well, I couldn't have been more wrong. I immediately became the holiday pariah. My Airbnb was considered gratuitous and profligate. It was also 'miles from Mum's' (for the record, it was fourteen houses away in the same street). And except for the master bedroom and en suite, the entire house went unused. No meals were cooked in that kitchen, no ablutions were performed in the main bathroom, even the TV went unused. In fact, my own partner only stopped by, reluctantly, in the evenings to sleep and to shower. As soon as the sun rose, he was straight down to Mum's for bunk-in breakfast with the gang.

The following year we broke up, right before Bunk-in, and he went to Mum's without me. I wasn't missed. To be honest, I'm not convinced anyone else even realised we'd broken up —they probably all just assumed I was 'miles away', holed up in my lavish and unnecessary house down the road.

---------------------------→

HOUSEGUESTS

413
Three days only

This is not my rule by the way—this is accepted worldwide as standard. It's also ignored worldwide as standard.

I don't mind people coming to stay; I have a spare bedroom so no one has to bunk in and I rather like having friends visit me. Three days is completely tolerable. However, after three days everyone starts to get on your tits. For three days, you can put up with people not putting their breakfast comestibles away or leaving half-drunk cups of tea around your house or using all the hot water or putting dishes in the sink instead of the dishwasher. But any more than three days of that behaviour and they start to feel like a shitty flatmate rather than a guest.

414
Don't dominate the shared living spaces

This is particularly important if you are a young, male houseguest. As mentioned earlier, youths have an almost superhuman ability to spread themselves and take up all available space. A lounge that would normally accommodate three adults comfortably, looks positively crowded with only two youths on it.

415
Never come home empty-handed

Think of the money you are saving on accommodation and parlay that into a series of small gifts. After all, you'll only be there for three days, so that's not too much to ask. Basically, you should be proffering a token of appreciation each day, be it a bottle of wine or some nice fruit or a box of Paddlepops for the kids. This goes a long way to keeping your hosts happy and, more importantly, ensures they will have you back again rather than inventing some vague excuse as to why you can't stay next time. If you ever hear something like this, 'Oh no, sorry, that week doesn't work for us because um ... yeah ... it just doesn't. Maybe next time,' you know you've been a dud houseguest.

416
Leave on the day you said you would leave

A favourite trick of people who like free accommodation is to announce a change of circumstance mid-stay and then put the host on the spot by saying, 'Oh my flight was cancelled' or 'My other accommodation fell through', and then asking if they can stay an extra day or two. This fools no one. Your host knows what you're doing; they know that you know it's impossible to say no to your face, especially once you're already ensconced in the house. But while you might squeeze out a few extra nights on this visit, it's not really worth it because you risk being barred from any future stays.

VISITORS TO OUR SHORES

417
Don't plonk your towel uncomfortably close to someone else's

This should be the only question on an Australian citizenship test: *At the beach, how much space should you leave between your towel and that of a stranger?*

The answer is a minimum of one and a half metres, and that is if the beach is packed; if it's not packed, then anything less than three metres is encroachment bordering on harassment. There should be at least a whole towel-length of clear space between one group and the next.

If you were viewing the beach from the air, what you should see is a whole lot of multicoloured clusters of towels broken up by clear wide sand perimeters around each group. Australians have large beaches and plenty of them, there is always space, you might just need to walk a bit further up the beach to find it. Don't be lazy, keep walking.

418
Vegemite is no big deal

It's just salty. And to any visiting celebrities, perhaps tell your publicist to ban 'journalists' from asking you whether you've tried it yet. This is not for your sake—as I said, there's nothing wrong with Vegemite—it's more for the sake of the Australian viewing public. We are all sick to death of excitable journos asking celebs, 'Have you tried Vegemite? Oh my god! What did you think of it?!' No one cares. And for the record, a lot of Australians don't like it either. (I'm not one of them by the way, I love the stuff.)

ART & ENTERTAINMENT

A word about 'culture'

Most of us happily ignore galleries and museums until we are overseas, when we are suddenly struck by an overwhelming and oppressive obligation to do things we would never normally do, like visit museums and art galleries.

Friends of mine are appalled when I admit that I don't really want to queue up to go to MoMA or the Guggenheim or even the Louvre. I'm not against art or old stuff, I'm simply not into queuing. If I could just wander in for a quick squizz when I happened to be in the area, I'd do it for sure, but that's not an option. Places are so busy now, you have to plan your visit in advance, which usually includes pre-purchasing your ticket. However, even with a pre-purchased ticket you still have to queue up to get inside and then, once inside, you are herded through the halls and exhibits by staff barking at you to 'Keep moving folks, keep moving!' It's just not a fun day out when you factor in all the queuing and the yelling, especially when the only reward is a room full of old bowls and spoons and bits of flint.

These days I tend to travel mostly with my sister because she holds no truck with galleries and museums either. She is unapologetic about the fact that she would rather go for lunch at a diner or spend an afternoon shopping at Bloomingdale's than shuffle around a museum pretending to be fascinated by armless statues and ancient ewers. She would rather have a cocktail in a bar with a view **of** the Empire State Building than queue to go **up** the Empire State Building and then look down at the many places below where one could be enjoying a cocktail.

But if you can't avoid it and you find yourself being dragged around an art gallery or museum, you will no doubt benefit from the following rules.

MUSEUMS AND ART GALLERIES

419
It is worth queuing for a natural history museum

I realise I just said I don't like queuing, but I make an exception for natural history museums because I really like dinosaur skeletons and I'm fascinated by things preserved in jars of formaldehyde. Also you get to see a whole bunch of creepy taxidermied creatures that, for some reason, are always posed so as to appear threatening. Even the sweetest-looking little desert mouse becomes menacing when he's stuffed and stood on his hind legs with his little pointy teeth bared. I wish that was an option for people. I don't really fancy being buried or cremated but I'd love to be stuffed and placed in an exhibit at the Natural History museum; I could be posed sitting cross-legged, mouth slightly open, staring glassy-eyed at a television, a true representation of the 21st-century human.

420
Stand well back from the exhibit

It's an artwork not the baggage carousel. Don't bunch around it and prevent others from getting a decent look.

421
Don't take photos of a painting

Taking a photo of a famous painting on your phone is almost as stupid as going to a live concert and filming it instead of watching it. When has anyone ever sat down to watch the brilliant concert footage they filmed on their iPhone from Row W? If a painting is so famous that you want a picture of it, there's every chance you'll be able to find a much better image online or in postcard form at the gift shop on the way out. Trust me, no one wants to look at your bad photo of a painting. A painting which is probably behind glass anyway so all you've really managed to capture are the reflections of other people gathered around taking photos of the painting.

Seriously, there's no need to take pictures of pictures. It's really dumb.

422
Go with someone who has the same boredom threshold as you

The minute I set foot in a gallery or museum, I check my watch and start thinking about how long I have to wait before I can suggest we find the cafe and have coffee and cake. I usually last about fifteen minutes, which means I need to be with a friend who has the same low tolerance level as me, because when I turn around and say, 'Should we get cake?' I want an enthusiastic thumbs up, not a withering look that tells me I'm an uncultured swine with no appreciation of fine art.

423
Think twice before purchasing in the gift shop

I understand everyone likes a souvenir, at the very least you want something that reminds you of the time you queued for two hours in order to get into the Louvre where you quite possibly motored your way directly to the *Mona Lisa* and came straight back out again. (No judgement from me.)

Once you are in the gift shop, however, it's easy to get a bit giddy and over-excited—for a start, it means you're almost out of there—but don't get carried away. Stop and consider the artist for a moment when you're browsing through the endless merchandise available. Ask yourself, is it what da Vinci would have wanted? His artwork printed on a tote bag that will be used to cart around your stinky yoga clothes? His artwork on a beach towel that will be used to rub down a half-naked, salty, sandy person? Maybe just buy a postcard—it's bound to be better than that photograph you took on your phone.

424
Not all of your thoughts need to be articulated

This is a rule for a certain type of tourist (often American but not always) who doesn't seem to understand that it's okay for some of your thoughts to remain in your head. No need to provide a running commentary on everything you're seeing and doing. Perhaps just try seeing and doing. For example, when I went to see the Book of Kells exhibition at Trinity College Library in Dublin, there were many other people enjoying the display in silence. Only Harry and Lorraine from Iowa felt the need to play a loud game of 'say what you see' as they waddled around the hall. Here are a few fun facts Lorraine felt she should share with everyone else in the room, just in case we were all illiterate and couldn't read the same information panel she was now reading.

'Monks wrote this book? Monks? Can you believe it, Harry? It was monks!?'

Lorraine was so impressed by the fact that monks wrote the book that I started to wonder whether she thought 'monks' was actually an Irish word for monkeys. She was then struck by something else incredibly fascinating.

'They wrote it by heee-yand [hand], Harry, this whole book, all by heee-yand, can you believe it?' For some reason she seemed surprised that these ninth-century monks (or monkeys?) weren't using Microsoft Word.

Basically, the rule is, not every thought has to be vocalised and it certainly doesn't have to be vocalised at volume.

THE ZOO

I realise that zoos are a contentious issue —none of us likes to think about wild animals being kept in cages. That said, I just love animals so much that if there's a chance to see some, even if they're in cages, I'll take it. When I am on tour, if I have time, I like to seek out the local zoo and go look at animals. Any animals. I even like the boring, smelly mountain goats, the way they stand awkwardly on top of rocky outcrops and seem to have no other purpose in life but to cover the ground with their pellety poo. As for meerkats, I can watch those things for hours. But my favourite exhibit of all time has to be the African painted dogs at the Perth Zoo. Nice one Perth Zoo, double thumbs up.

And while I have always enjoyed the city of Wagga Wagga (they have some excellent restaurants and cafes and a terrific arts centre), I must say they are drawing a very long bow in claiming to have a zoo. But claim they do. It's listed prominently on the visitor information leaflet and there are quite a few signs up around the town directing you to the Wagga Wagga Zoo. The problem is, there's no zoo. There's a peacock, a pig and a couple of ducks. So my first rule is:

425

Birds plus a farm animal does not maketh a zoo

It's not just Wagga—a lot of small towns claim to have a zoo when all they have is a sheep, a goat (regular not mountain) and a few geese. Technically, that's a small farm. To be classified as a zoo, you must have something larger than a cow, like an elephant. Or something that can eat you, like a bear or a lion.

And no, I'm afraid exotic birds don't count—that's an aviary, not a zoo. If it's a place that only has native Australian animals, that's okay but maybe call it a 'wildlife sanctuary', so I can lower my expectations before I get there. For example, 'Tamworth Marsupial Park' leaves prospective guests in no doubt as to what they should expect. And it really makes a difference. I went in expecting marsupials, I got those critters in spades, and I enjoyed my visit immensely. Five stars.

426
No talking

Before I get called a Grinch, this is a rule for adults not children. Children sound a lot like chattering monkeys when they are excited, and that's completely appropriate at the zoo, therefore I have no problem with it. It's the endless and senseless educational monologuing from parents at the zoo that I find tedious. At every single exhibit you are forced to listen to adults jabbering away, trying to turn a fun day out at the zoo into a series of teachable moments. 'Do you know what this animal is, Jacob? It's a lion. What noise does a lion make? Can you roar like a lion, Jacob? Can you see the lion? Do you think he might be hiding?'

I guarantee you the lion is hiding, Jacob, inside his cave with his paws over his ears, rocking back and forth, going, 'Make it stop, Jacob, please make the grown-up stop talking!'

The zoo is already fun, there is already plenty to do and see, so relax, mum and dad, dial down the audible parenting. You've done your job by bringing the child to a stimulating environment, you don't need to constantly badger them with questions and knowledge and learning.

427
No tapping

This is a rule for both adults and children. Zoos have a way of bringing out the dumbest behaviour in humans. It's as if this visual reminder that we are at the top of the food chain makes us so arrogant that we forget how to behave in a civilised fashion— from tapping on the glass to 'wake' up the animals to climbing into enclosures in order to get a selfie with a bear. If you get eaten at the zoo because you climbed over a fence, that's called natural selection and the world won't miss you.

THE THEATRE

428
Leave at interval if you're not enjoying it

If the play is rubbish in the first half, it's unlikely it will suddenly pick up in the second half, so it's perfectly acceptable to cut your losses and leave at interval. You're actually doing the producers a service as it's the only discreet way to send a message that the play is not up to scratch and needs work.

The problem is theatre audiences are incredibly polite and invariably they will still clap at the end of a play whether it's good or bad. And because all clapping sounds the same, the actors have no way of telling whether the applause indicates enjoyment or simply relief that the play is over.

Comedians are possibly the only performers who constantly get honest feedback. When audiences don't enjoy comedy, they don't laugh, which is a clear indicator to the comedian that they are not being funny. Sometimes an audience member will go even further and actually yell out exactly what they think of the comedian. And while it can be alarming to be told that 'you're shit!' it's also the quickest way to learn not to be shit. Playwrights and actors don't enjoy the benefit of that kind of honest feedback so a walkout at interval is the kindest thing you can do for them.

BOOKS

429
Never tell someone the book (or movie) has a twist

This ruins the whole book, because the person then spends their whole time reading, thinking, *Ooh, I wonder if this is the twist?*

430
Don't say you hate Kindles because you 'love the smell of books'

If you're such a big reader you should have a lower tolerance for clichés.

431
If you borrow a book, return it promptly

Conversely, if you lend someone a book, be prepared never to see it again.

432
Don't recommend award-winning literature to make yourself appear smart

If you genuinely enjoyed it, by all means pass on your recommendation, but don't just pretend you liked it because you think you will sound dumb if you admit you didn't really get it and that you found the language incredibly dense to the point of being impenetrable.

433
Don't talk in the library

Another stupidly obvious rule; however, I am including it, not so much for the library users, but more for the library staff themselves. Library staff used to be aggressive in their pursuit of silence, stalking around the book stacks and appearing out of nowhere to angrily shush anyone who dared to so much as whisper. Now, they don't even admonish people who are talking on their phones and they certainly don't try to stop anyone from munching on noisy foodstuffs like crisps and corn chips. Worse than that, these days it's often the staff members themselves who are the main offenders. It's like they've decided they are above the law and the no talking rule does not apply to them. There are a couple of staff members at my local library who positively bellow every time someone approaches the desk to get some information. Apparently they don't teach 'hushed tones' and 'monotone mumbling' at librarian school anymore.

SPECIAL REMOVABLE SECTION
REALITY TELEVISION

Reality TV is more popular now than ever before, which is aston-ishing. I naively assumed that once people had seen reality TV and realised how it works, these shows would disappear from our screens. Because surely after you've seen a show like The Bachelor *or* My Kitchen Rules *or* Married at First Sight *and watched how people are portrayed as either idiots or arseholes (or sometimes both) you couldn't possibly be convinced to sign up for one. I figured that by season three of any reality show they'd be forced to cast Amish folk because they'd be the only people in the world oblivious to the machinations of shows like* Twenty Desperate Women in Polyester Frocks Competing for One Incredibly Dull Man in a Tuxedo.

Turns out, I'm like Jon Snow, I know nothing. And in fact, applications for these shows are on the rise. Where once the standard response to, 'Would you like to go on television, be made to look stupid, have the worst side of yourself on display and be publicly humiliated?' would have been 'No thanks, I'd rather be dead', these days, more and more people are up for it. Apparently, the lure of Insta fame, at whatever price, is too attractive.

So if you happen to know one of these bizarre individuals who aspires to be on reality TV, feel free to remove this section from the book and give it to them. It might help them to avoid looking like a total dick. The key word there is 'might'. There are no guarantees. Very few people come out of these shows looking good, which brings us nicely to the most important rule of reality television:

434
The producer is not your friend

Never forget that, not even for a minute. Off screen, they'll pretend to care, they'll pretend to be your buddy, but on screen you are going to be stitched up and presented as either contempt-ible or crazy. The producers will always find a way to make you look stupid, whether it's through guile, fatigue or just plying you with alcohol.

Even if you do manage to keep it together during filming, even if you stay alert and keep yourself nice, even if you don't give producers what they want on tape, they will find a way to get you in the edit. You can't win. The only sure-fire way to beat the producer and come out looking like a decent person, is to say, 'No, I do not wish to participate in this program.'

435
Have a cracking backstory

Whatever show you're going on, make sure you have a backstory that involves either something sad, like an ailing grandmother, or something titillating, like escaping from a cult. It will not only guarantee you get cast but it will also make it harder for people to hate you on social media. People will still find a way to hate you on social media, but at least you'll make it more difficult for them.

LOVE SHOWS

436
Never say 'I have a lot of love to give'

Sounding off about having a lot of love to give makes it sound like you have a virulent STD just waiting to be transferred. Or that you have a massive surplus of love because no one has ever wanted to take it from you.

437
Avoid the clichés

The most tiresome cliché trotted out on these shows is the one where someone says they are 'afraid to open up because they've been hurt before'. This is complete poppycock. The real reason that person is not opening up is because they are not in any way attracted to the love object on offer.

The right thing to do in this instance is stop boring us with your trite soundbites, admit the other person doesn't blow your skirt up and exit the show. Unless, of course, you didn't *actually* go on the show to find love? But who would do that?

438
Don't mention your walls

There are more references to walls on *The Bachelor* and *Married at First Sight* than there are on *The Block*. Everyone has their walls up these days. Maybe that's why they've all got 'so much love to give'—it's been piling up behind those walls unable to escape. But I'm afraid you can't talk about having your walls up while simultaneously allowing dozens of cameras to film everything you do and say.

439
No need to mention how important your kids are to you

Especially when you've just abandoned them for an indefinite period of time in order to follow your dream of becoming a celebrity by appearing on a reality TV show—a show where your kids will get to watch you behave like an undignified tit, say embarrassing things and quite possibly open-mouth kiss a stranger on national television. If you really love your kids, don't search for a new partner on a reality TV show.

RENOVATION SHOWS

440
Stop installing black tapware

Honestly, that stuff is going to look dated before this book has even hit the shelves. Same goes for rose gold tapware.

441
No stupid giant overhead shower roses

Women hate them. They might look much more fancy than a standard shower head on an adjustable arm but they're really annoying because the water just rains down all over your head, which means you have to wear a shower cap every time.

442
You can't improve on the light switch

Imagine this scenario: you walk into a room, it's dark, you flick a switch on the wall, the room lights up. Magic. The light switch is one of the greatest inventions of all time, the very definition of practicality and functionality. And yet contestants on renovation shows are always desperate to replace light switches with complicated technology like C-Bus or those creepy Alexa Google robot things? I can't see what advantage is gained by entering a room and shouting (slowly and deliberately) into the air, 'Alexa—turn—on—my—living—room—light!' It's no faster than flicking a switch. It's lazy, in that you literally can't be bothered lifting a finger, not to mention it's also advocating bad manners, because no one ever says 'please' or 'thank you' when they order Alexa the Google Robot to turn on the lights. All up it seems to indicate people's impolitic desire to return to the days of having servants and slaves to do your bidding for you.

443
No one needs a 'reading landing'

A reading landing is a bit of a wank. It's actually just a flat bit at the top of the stairs furnished with a comfy chair that no one will ever sit on and a bookshelf filled with books that no one will ever read.

COOKING SHOWS

First of all, let me say I am impressed by anyone who can cook under pressure and within a certain timeframe. While I am fairly confident that I could attempt any recipe, I would need all day to do it. And there's no way I could cook with a clock counting down and judges yelling at me that my time was nearly up. I'd have a meltdown and end up in the foetal position on the bench with my head in a George Foreman grill. So I admire anyone who can cook under time pressure (which, I guess when you think about it, is pretty much any decent chef in a decent restaurant).

444
Cook with ingredients and utensils

Every season we see a slew of contestants who claim to 'cook with love' and then wonder why they don't win the show. I've made plenty of cakes in my time, some good, some okay, some disastrous. And with regard to those baking disasters, the problem always came down to my not paying enough attention to the recipe or not being precise enough with my measurements. Throwing in an extra cup of love would not have made a jot of difference.

It's the same when friends come over for dinner. Sometimes they ask for the salt or the pepper, but no one has ever said, 'Kitty, this mutton stew is really unpleasant, I think it needs more love? Do you have any love in your pantry? Don't get up, just tell me where it is, I'll get it.'

445
If in doubt, roll Nonna out

Even if you didn't have a nonna that sat you on her lap and taught you how to roll pasta or make cannoli, invent one, especially if you think you're about to flame out in a challenge. Take your food up to the tasting bench and tell them it's your grandmother's secret recipe and that it's a traditional dish passed down over generations. The judges never trash old ladies' recipes, especially when they're from another country; it would make them seem culturally ignorant or insensitive.

446
Stop saying your dream is to open a dessert bar

Dessert bars are only a good idea on paper or *maybe* in New York where there are millions of people and the city never sleeps (TM Frank Sinatra). But not in Australia. For a start, no one wants to move venues to have dessert. Changing venues kills the vibe. Also, the minute you try to move a group en masse, you lose people. Once everyone is out on the street debating the best way to get to this dessert bar—'Can we walk? How far is it? Do we need two cabs?'—it all becomes too hard and people just go home.

And for people like me who often finish work late and have trouble finding a restaurant that is still open and serving food (because I live in Sydney, an international city, where restaurant kitchens close at 9 pm), the dessert bar is a cruel illusion. The doors are open, the lights are on, it looks like food is still being served, so you start to think you might actually be able to get a meal, only to walk in and be crushed by the news that 'Yes, we are still serving but ... we only do desserts.'

THE FINAL RULE

447
Lower your expectations, that way you can never be disappointed

Some of you may have been expecting a few more rules—after all, it says 488 on the cover. Honestly though, I'm amazed and also slightly alarmed that I made it this far. I knew I had a lot of rules but I had no idea I had this many.

If you're wondering why the book wasn't called *447 Rules for Life*, I did mention in the introduction that this book started life as a joke, it was never supposed to be anything more than a funny title. Once it became a real book, I decided I really liked the number 488 and didn't want to change it.

And since embarking on this project and discussing it with everyone I meet, I've discovered that everybody has a rule about something. I guarantee that the minute you finish this book you will, no doubt, start thinking of other rules I should have included.

Hang on, there was no rule about how often you should change the sheets?

or

Why didn't she include a rule about not putting parmesan cheese on seafood pasta?

or

Seriously? No rule about always wiping front to back. She's dead to me.

So these last few pages are for you, the owner of this compendium, to fill in whatever rules you think I have omitted. They can be completely logical or totally insane. You'll get no judgement from me, in fact I promise to endorse any and all additions, no matter how nutty. Add as many as you like because one rule I admit I did forget to include is that you can never have too many rules.

INSERT YOUR OWN RULES FOR LIFE

Acknowledgements

The first person who gets a thankyou is obviously Mr Jordan Peterson. It's no secret his book inspired mine—I'm just glad he stopped at twelve and left the rest for me.

I need to thank the fabulous ladies at Allen & Unwin: Kelly Fagan for pushing me to write this book and Angela Handley for pushing me to stop writing this book and finish it already; thank you, Angela, you've been incredibly patient.

Thanks to my fellow rule-makers, Sophie, Penny and Rozie, not only for your excellent contributions but also for helping to keep this book from becoming the insane rantings of a middle-aged lady. (I hope.)

Bruce Griffiths always deserves my thanks, for suggestions, contributions and for being someone who loves rules as much as I do.

To my best friend Glenn, thank you for sharing the knowledge on what it takes to be a good conversationalist and for generously participating in the many tour-van chats I hijacked and made all about me and my rules book.

Thanks to Nina Oyama, for being my totally shmood youth-speak consultant. (I know, I know, I'm not using shmood correctly.)

Tom Peterson, my producer on *The Weekly*, thank you for the brilliant job you did on the 488 Rules segment, you made people want a book that didn't exist. Well played.

To Tohby Riddle, who designed the book and did the illustrations. You're such a class act and the best kind of perfectionist. I heart you.

Thank you to my dad, who assured me that no one ever turns their book in on time and said I wasn't to let anyone rush me. (This from a man who has never missed a deadline.)

Nothing I do would be possible without the support of A-List Management—Artie Laing, you are a diamond, and Karen Laing, please promise you will never leave me.

Finally, to Joel, my unicorn, thank you for always being so incredibly supportive. I don't know how you tolerate so many rules yet somehow you do—well, except for number 191. But I know you're working on that one, and I appreciate it. xx